THE TRUTH ABOUT GERONIMO

GERONIMO

THE TRUTH ABOUT
GERONIMO

BY

BRITTON DAVIS

EDITED BY

M. M. QUAIFE

WITH A FOREWORD BY ROBERT M. UTLEY

UNIVERSITY OF NEBRASKA PRESS
LINCOLN and LONDON

Manufactured in the United States of America

First Bison Book printing: 1976

Most recent printing indicated by first digit below:
2 3 4 5 6 7 8 9 10

Bison Book edition reproduced from the second printing (July 1963) by arrangement with Yale University Press.

Library of Congress Cataloging in Publication Data

Davis, Britton, 1860–
The truth about Geronimo.

"A Bison book."
Reprint of the 1929 ed. published by Yale University Press, New Haven.
1. Geronimo, Apache chief, 1829–1909. 2. Apache Indians—Wars, 1883–1886. I. Title.
E99.A6G323 1976 970'.004'97 [B] 75–37958
ISBN 0–8032–0877–4
ISBN 0–8032–5840–2 pbk.

IN MEMORY

of my former comrades, the late Emmet Crawford, Captain Third U.S. Cavalry; Charles B. Gatewood, First Lieutenant Sixth U.S. Cavalry; and those others of the Army of the West who "carried on" with no thought of reward for performance of duty.

Foreword

BY ROBERT M. UTLEY

GENERAL George Crook believed that it took an Indian to catch an Indian, and when possible he conducted his campaigns on this principle. Although few of his fellow officers repudiated the regulars so fully, Indian auxiliaries played an increasingly important role in the frontier warfare of the 1880s. For a time in the 90s, the Crook doctrine attained its fullest expression, with the incorporation of one Indian company into each regiment of cavalry and infantry. Much more than the regulars, these native soldiers demanded the highest type of leadership, and commanders usually assigned their most promising young lieutenants to the scout units. In this manner, there emerged in the Army a small corps of able officers whose specialty was the management of Indians. It was a specialty that few whites possessed, and it qualified the scout leaders as experts on the "Indian problem" that so vexed nineteenth-century America. The roll of scout commanders bore names that figure prominently in the annals of the Indian-fighting Army—Ezra P. Ewers, Hugh L. Scott, Homer W. Wheeler, Edward W. Casey, Emmet Crawford, Charles B. Gatewood, and the author of the following narrative, Britton Davis.

Many actors in the drama of Indian warfare wrote accounts of their experiences, but the observations of men like Britton Davis cast a much brighter illumination on the essential nature of the drama than those of an ordinary troop commander. Living with their native charges in the intimacy of camp and field, the scout officers acquired a knowledge, an understanding, and a sympathy for the American Indian that few others could match. Equipped with an insight into the workings of the Indian mind as well as the military mind, those who set their experiences to paper achieved a degree of perception rare in contemporary accounts of the conflict.

In conversation with artist Frederic Remington, an officer of long experience with Indian scouts revealed why Britton Davis and his colleagues were of such value to the Army and at the same time so well fitted to aid later generations to understand what the Indian wars were really like. "I have lived with Indians for years and years at a time," he said, "and I suppose if I died, the papers would say, 'He was a great Indian fighter.' In reality I have been in only a few small affairs of that character, but I have done a power of Indian thinking for which I will receive no credit. It would often be better and more truthful to call us 'Indian thinkers' rather than 'fighters.' "[1]

Britton Davis was one of these Indian thinkers. Moreover, he brought other qualifications to the task of relating the truth about Geronimo. He was a participant in many of the significant episodes of the Apache troubles and hovered close enough on the fringes of others to gain first-hand knowledge of what had happened. He knew the principal figures on both sides—Geronimo, Chato, Chihuahua, Natchez (Nachite according to Davis), Crook, Crawford, Gatewood, Sieber, and the rest of that cast of colorful characters who made frontier Arizona such an exciting corner of the American West. Finally, when he sat down years later to write his story, Davis kept on the desk before him the written accounts of fellow officers and much of the official correspondence that flowed through Army channels during the Geronimo campaign. These papers succeeded remarkably in clarifying a memory that might otherwise have dimmed. The historian who checks *The Truth about Geronimo* against other first-hand evidence finds Davis wrong in few places. The narrative, furthermore, is fast paced and often highly suspenseful. It is one of the best books, both as source and as literature, to come from the frontier. This was true in 1929, when the Yale University Press published the first edition; it is equally true today.

Britton Davis was born in Brownsville, Texas, on June 4, 1860,

1. Quoted in "How an Apache War Was Won," in Harold McCracken, ed., *Frederic Remington's Own West* (New York, Dial Press, 1961), p. 49.

the son of Edmund J. Davis, prominent lawyer and judge of the judicial district bordering the lower Rio Grande. When Britton (his mother's maiden name) was a year old, the Civil War burst on the nation. Defeated in the election for delegate from his district to the Texas Secession Convention, Judge Davis repaired to the Mexican side of the river and organized a regiment of Texas Unionists, which he commanded in the Louisiana campaigns throughout the conflict. Emerging from the war a brigadier general, he plunged into the morass of Reconstruction politics in Texas and swiftly rose to the leadership of the Radical Republicans.

Backed by the Army, the Radicals triumphed over the Moderate Republicans, and Davis was elected governor of Texas in 1869. Supported by a negro state police, he reigned as a virtual dictator for four years and, although defeated in 1873, relinquished office only after President Grant refused to support his pretensions. Although his administration was riddled with incompetent and dishonest appointees, the governor himself seems to have retained a reputation for ability and sincerity, and his home life, in which his son grew to maturity, was one of culture and refinement.[2] Britton Davis entered the United States Military Academy at West Point on September 1, 1877, and was graduated forty-fourth in his class four years later. Appointed second lieutenant in the Third Cavalry in June 1881, he was posted to Troop L at Fort D. A. Russell, Wyoming.[3]

Lieutenant Davis arrived in Arizona in the summer of 1882 just as the last phase of the conflict between the United States and the Chiricahua Apaches was beginning. Of all the Apache groups that impeded the advance of the southwestern frontier, the Chiricahuas had proved the most tenacious in their opposition. The able Cochise had led his people in a relentless war that lasted from 1860 until 1872, when Gen. Oliver O. Howard and

2. *Dictionary of American Biography, 5,* 112-13.

3. F. B. Heitman, *Historical Register and Dictionary of the United States Army* (2 vols. Washington, 1903), *1,* 357.

Tom Jeffords made peace with him. After the death of Cochise in 1874, the chieftainship fell to his elder son Taza. Two years later these people were moved from their beloved Chiricahua Mountains to the San Carlos Agency, in the parched bottomlands of the Gila River, where the Government intended to colonize all the Arizona Apaches. Some of the Chiricahuas had chosen fugitive life instead. Under Juh, Noglee, and a rising leader named Geronimo, these "renegades" ravaged Arizona, Chihuahua, and Sonora until 1879, when they, too, were persuaded to settle at San Carlos. On the reservation, white encroachment and blundering administration combined with discontent over the loss of their homeland to keep the Chiricahuas constantly unsettled. Taza lacked the force of his father, and Natchez, younger son of Cochise, who succeeded to the chieftainship after the death of his brother, exerted even less leadership. Geronimo led the renegades in another outbreak in 1881 and again took refuge in the mountain recesses of Mexico.

A powerful stocky warrior with a perpetual scowl on his face, Geronimo personified all that was savage and cruel in the Apache. Although not a chief, he built up a respectable following through force of personality and opposition to the white man's rule. Few whites who knew him had much praise for him, and most of his own people feared and disliked him. Davis characterized him as "a thoroughly vicious, intractable, and treacherous man. His only redeeming traits were courage and determination. His word, no matter how earnestly pledged, was worthless." History has supported this judgment.

Davis' transfer from Wyoming to Arizona was part of the Army's response to the Geronimo outbreak of 1881. Brig. Gen. George Crook had proved in the brilliant Tonto Basin campaign of 1872-73 that he knew how to fight Apaches. Such was his reputation that the nation at large joined the War Department in believing that if anyone could end the Apache war Crook was the man, and once more he was assigned to command the Department of Arizona. From the northern Plains he brought with him

Britton Davis' regiment, the Third Cavalry, which had served him in Arizona a decade earlier. In the same month that Davis reached Arizona, July 1882, the United States and Mexico signed an accord that permitted troops of either nation to cross the international boundary when in close pursuit of hostile Indians.[4] Thus Crook was free to track the renegades to their strongholds high in the Sierra Madre of Sonora and Chihuahua.

Plodding around the territory on his celebrated mule Apache, Crook held many councils with the Indians who had not fled to Mexico. He quickly concluded that they had been robbed, cheated, and abused by Indian agents, traders, and contractors; in fact, he reported, the Apaches had "displayed remarkable forebearance in remaining at peace."[5] No victory could be final, he knew, so long as conditions on the reservation were bad. The general thus waged his offensive on two fronts—in Mexico and on the San Carlos Reservation. It was on the latter front that Britton Davis first served.

Before plunging into the wilds of northern Mexico, Crook reorganized the administration of San Carlos. In November 1882 he called the reservation Indians into council and explained the new system. No longer would they have to live near the agency and report frequently for roll call. Henceforth they could settle wherever on the reservation they chose. Now that they could seek out better land, however, they would be expected to make a serious attempt at farming. Although the civilian agent and his staff would continue to perform their duties, the Indians would also be accountable to military agents—Capt. Emmet Crawford at San Carlos and Lt. Charles B. Gatewood at Fort Apache, to the north. Lt. Britton Davis was assigned to assist Crawford and Lt. Hamilton Roach to assist Gatewood. These officers were to recruit and command companies of Apache scouts to preserve the

4. U.S. Statutes at Large, *22*, 934.

5. Secretary of War, *Annual Report* (1883), p. 160.

peace. They were detached from their regiments and placed on General Crook's staff.[6]

While Davis labored to make soldiers out of Apaches at San Carlos, as narrated in Chapters 3 and 4, Crook campaigned in Mexico. Crossing the border early in May 1883 with 193 Apache scouts under Crawford and a troop of the Sixth Cavalry under Capt. Adna R. Chaffee, he combed the rugged wilderness of the Sierra Madre and on May 15 attacked the ranchería of Chato. That the mountains of Mexico no longer afforded a refuge came as a surprising revelation to the fugitive chiefs; one by one Chihuahua, Chato, Natchez, and even Geronimo came in and declared their desire to be forgiven. The means by which the hostiles were returned to San Carlos is described by Davis in Chapters 5 and 6.[7]

Most of the newly surrendered Apaches took advantage of Crook's policy of allowing them to live where they wished on the reservation, and they moved into the cool pine forests of the Mogollon Rim north of San Carlos. Davis' scouts camped on Turkey Creek to watch them, and the lieutenant thus observed at close range the forces that brought about their last outbreak. It was the old story of divided authority. Although the War and Interior Departments had concluded a joint memorandum giving Crook police control of the San Carlos Indians,[8] the civil and military agents were constantly at odds. Restless, resenting the prohibition of such time-honored customs as wife-beating and tizwin-drinking, the Apaches sought to play off one agent against the other and became increasingly defiant of all authority. Davis was a key figure in the outbreak of May 17, 1885, and describes it in Chapter 9. Geronimo, Natchez, and Nana led forty-two warriors and ninety-two women and children in a dash for the border.

6. Ibid. Frank C. Lockwood, *The Apache Indians* (New York, Macmillan, 1936), p. 261.

7. See also *Annual Report* (1883), pp. 173-78. John G. Bourke, *On the Border with Crook* (New York, Scribner, 1891), pp. 452-54. Martin F. Schmitt, ed., *General George Crook: His Autobiography* (Norman, University of Oklahoma Press, 1946), pp. 246-58.

8. Secretary of War, *Annual Report* (1882), p. 179.

Columns from Forts Bowie, Thomas, Huachuca, Grant, and Bayard tried to cut off the flight, but the fugitives, with their masterful evasive tactics, slipped safely across the border and lost themselves in the mountains.[9]

Crook conducted the campaign of 1885-86 in the same manner as that of 1882. He sent two columns of Apache scouts, provisioned by mule trains, south into Mexico. One was under Capt. Wirt Davis, with Gatewood as lieutenant; Crawford led the other, with Britton Davis assisting. The columns scoured the Sierra Madre, keeping the hostiles always on the move and always haunted by a feeling of insecurity. For scouts as well as officers, it was a fearful ordeal. It lasted throughout the summer of 1885 and so exhausted the pursuers that they limped back across the border early in the autumn.[10]

At this point Davis' direct participation in the campaign ends. He resigned from the Army and became the manager of a ranch in northwestern Chihuahua. But his account, carried through to the final surrender of Geronimo, loses none of its interest. For Davis now becomes an advocate—and an able one—in the fascinating controversy over who deserves the credit for the surrender of Geronimo. Were Crook's methods, particularly his heavy reliance on Indian scouts, consistent with sound military doctrine? Did Crook's superiors place him in a position that left him no honorable choice but to ask to be relieved from command? Did Crook's successor, Miles, arrange for his protégé Lawton to reap rewards for the final triumph that rightfully belonged to Gatewood, a protégé of Crook? The rapid rise of Lawton and the eclipse of Gatewood gave point to the questions, as did Miles' treatment of the Geronimo campaign in his widely read memoirs. Davis and others answer these questions in the affirmative. As a

9. Ibid. (1886), pp. 147-48. Ralph H. Ogle. "Federal Control of the Western Apaches, 1848-1886," *New Mexico Historical Review, 15* (1940), 314-21.

10. Secretary of War, *Annual Report* (1886), pp. 149-51. Schmitt, pp. 256-57. H. W. Daly, "The Geronimo Campaign," *Arizona Historical Review, 3* (1930), 26-44. Daly was Crawford's packmaster.

result of their labors, most recent histories assign Gatewood and Crook an influential part in the surrender of Geronimo, but without detracting measurably from the truly significant parts played by Lawton and Miles.[11]

After the Mexican expedition in which Britton Davis took part ended without perceptible result in September 1885, Crook prepared a second expedition. Again Crawford and Wirt Davis with their scouts pushed southward into the Sierra Madre. About 200 miles below the border, Crawford picked up a fresh trail and followed it to a hidden camp. The occupants had discovered his approach and pulled out, but they sent in a woman to say that Geronimo and Natchez wished to parley. The talks did not take place, for the next morning, January 11, 1886, Mexican militia troops attacked the scout camp. Crawford fell in the first fire, mortally wounded, and only after two hours of fighting did his lieutenant, Marion P. Maus, succeed in convincing the Mexican officers of their mistake. Two days later, however, Maus kept the appointment with Geronimo and the other hostile leaders. They insisted on talking with Crook personally, and a conference was arranged.[12]

On March 25, 1886, Crook and his staff seated themselves with Geronimo and his lieutenants in a wooded ravine at Cañon de los

11. Miles' version, which inspired so much animosity among the friends of Gatewood and Crook, is in *Personal Recollections and Observations of General Nelson A. Miles* (Chicago and New York, Werner, 1896), chs. 36-40; and *Serving the Republic: Memoirs of the Civil and Military Life of Nelson A. Miles* (New York and London, Harper, 1911), chs. 11, 12. The case for Crook and Gatewood is set forth in Bourke, *On the Border with Crook,* chs. 38, 39; Anton Mazzanovich, *Trailing Geronimo* (3d ed. Hollywood, 1931), pp. 259-318; and Charles B. Gatewood, "The Surrender of Geronimo," *Arizona Historical Review, 4* (1931), 34-44.

12. Maus' report, Feb. 23, 1886, in Secretary of War, *Annual Report* (1886), pp. 155-60. See also Maus' narrative in Miles, *Personal Recollections,* pp. 450-67. Crawford's body was later brought to Fort Bowie and, escorted by Capt. John G. Bourke, taken to his home in Nebraska for interment. The State Department took up the matter of the attack with the Mexican Government. Far from acknowledging responsibility, Mexico denied that an attack had taken place and demanded indemnity payments from the United States for a long list of depredations alleged to have been committed by the scouts. Secretary of War, *Annual Report* (1886), p. 10.

Embudos, twelve miles south of the border. For three days the general and the Apache argued, Crook striving for an unconditional surrender. "If you stay out," he warned, "I'll keep after you and kill the last one, if it takes fifty years." Two of his most trusted scouts, Ka-e-ten-a and Alchise, circulated among their hostile kinsmen urging surrender. But the wary Geronimo would not accede to unconditional surrender, and Crook had to make concessions. He promised that if the Apaches gave up, they would be confined in the East, with their families, for not more than two years and then could return to the reservation. On March 27, Chihuahua, Natchez, and finally Geronimo each made a speech formally surrendering to Crook. Leaving Lieutenant Maus to escort the prisoners, Crook and his staff returned to Fort Bowie and wired the news of the surrender to Lt. Gen. Philip H. Sheridan, commanding the Army. It was premature. A trader had sold the Apaches a quantity of mescal, the fiery Mexican intoxicant of which they were so fond. They got drunk, and the night after Crook's departure Geronimo and Natchez led twenty men and thirteen women in a dash for the mountains. Chihuahua and Nana with about a dozen men and forty-seven women and children remained behind to be escorted to Fort Bowie.[13]

Even before news of Geronimo's escape reached Washington, Crook was in trouble with his superiors. President Grover Cleveland refused to approve anything short of unconditional surrender, and General Sheridan instructed Crook to reopen negotiations to secure such a surrender. He was to "take every precaution against the escape of the hostiles" and to "insure against further hostilities by completing the destruction of the hostiles unless these terms are accepted." In other words, the Indians who had surrendered upon certain conditions must now agree to unconditional surrender or be destroyed. "Crook was not the man to lie to anyone or deal treacherously by him," observed Captain

13. The transcript of the conference, with related correspondence, is published in Senate Documents, 51st Cong., 1st sess., No. 88. Davis includes much of it in Chs. 12 and 13. See also Bourke, pp. 478-79; and Schmitt, pp. 199-200.

Bourke. "Unless he treacherously murdered them in cold blood, he was unable to see a way out of the dilemma."[14] Then Sheridan learned that Geronimo and Natchez had fled to the mountains, and he bombarded Crook with petulant dispatches implying that the Apache scouts, whom Crook regarded as the only troops able to track down the renegades, were not only unreliable but disloyal as well. On April 1 Crook requested relief from his command. The next day Sheridan issued orders directing Brig. Gen. Nelson A. Miles to take over the Department of Arizona.

The new commanding general contrasted sharply with the old. Crook, modest and unassuming, had often given the impression of shyness. Miles, vain, pompous, and unabashedly ambitious, loved nothing more than playing to a packed grandstand. Crook detested military display and rarely donned a uniform unless the occasion demanded it. Miles gloried in martial panoply and made the most of the privileges due a brigadier general. Crook devoutly believed that Apaches could best be subdued by other Apaches. Miles agreed with Sheridan that native scouts were not to be trusted and that regulars ought to be given a chance to run down the renegades. He now had his chance to test this view. With 5,000 regulars, he faced the task of destroying or forcing the unconditional surrender of a mere handful of Apaches.

Like Crook, Miles sent columns into Mexico, but they were formed of regulars rather than Indian scouts. One elite command of specially selected men was organized and placed under Capt. Henry W. Lawton and Assistant Surgeon Leonard Wood. It consisted of a company of infantry, 35 cavalrymen (whose horses broke down within a week), 100 mules with 30 packers, and, as guides and trailers, 20 Indian scouts. For four months Lawton pursued the quarry from one mountain range to another. The 1400-mile trek forms a record of hardship and persistence that earned these troops a well-deserved place in military history. Only once, however, did they corner any Apaches. And then it was the Indian scouts who discovered the camp and led the regulars to it.

14. *On the Border with Crook,* pp. 483-84.

As the infantry moved into position on July 14, the Apaches took alarm and fled, leaving an empty camp as the only prize of the effort.[15]

While Lawton campaigned in Mexico, Miles initiated two other measures destined to prove consequential. The first was the removal of the reservation Chiricahuas; sooner or later, he believed, they would supply ammunition and recruits to their kindred on the warpath. After a lengthy exchange of telegrams with General Sheridan, he finally won authority to carry out the proposal. On August 29, 1886, the reservation Chiricahuas were summoned to Fort Apache for a routine roll call, swiftly surrounded by an overwhelming force of cavalry, and marched off to the railroad at Holbrook. There, 382 Indians, including most of the scouts who had served Crook, boarded a train for Fort Marion, Florida.[16]

The other measure was a peace overture. Miles rightly perceived that Lawton's unrelenting pursuit would make the hostiles receptive. In July, at Fort Apache, he selected two Chiricahuas, Kayitah and Martine, known to have influence with the fugitive leaders, and sent them into Mexico with Lieutenant Gatewood, whom Geronimo knew and respected.

After many adventures, the lieutenant and his Indians made contact with Geronimo on August 24, five days before the Chiricahua removal from Fort Apache. Gatewood delivered Miles' ultimatum: "Surrender, and you will be sent with your families to Florida, there to await the decision of the President as to your final disposition." Geronimo was willing to surrender if he could return to the reservation, but not if he had to go to Florida. Only after Gatewood dropped the disconcerting news that all the other Chiricahuas were even then being moved to Florida did Geronimo give in. The formal surrender to Miles himself took place at

15. For the details of Lawton's operations see his report, Sept. 9, 1886, in Secretary of War, *Annual Report* (1886), pp. 176-81; and Wood's narrative in Miles, *Personal Recollections*, pp. 505-17. Hermann Hagedorn, *Leonard Wood: A Biography* (2 vols. New York, 1931), *1*, 67-103, follows the expedition in detail, quoting freely from a diary Wood kept.

16. Secretary of War, *Annual Report* (1886), pp. 14-15, 73-74, 170-71.

Skeleton Canyon, sixty-five miles southeast of Fort Bowie, on September 4, 1886. Four days later the prisoners were assembled on the parade ground at Fort Bowie and, as the Fourth Cavalry band played "Auld Lang Syne," marched to Bowie Station, where they were loaded on a train and started for Florida.[17]

Geronimo and Natchez had surrendered, but the nation had not heard the last of the Chiricahuas. Neither had General Miles. President Cleveland, elated at the outcome of the campaign, wired Miles to hold the prisoners at Fort Bowie until they could be turned over to the Arizona civil authorities for criminal trial. Miles was in an embarrassing position. He had to explain to the President that, like Crook, he had not won an unconditional surrender. (The Apaches had been told that their lives would be spared and that they would be sent to Florida until the President decided what to do with them; this Gatewood had promised on Miles' authority, and this Miles himself had promised at Skeleton Canyon.) Moreover, the prisoners were no longer at Fort Bowie but already speeding toward Florida. The President promptly ordered them detained at San Antonio, Texas, until he could find out exactly what terms Miles had granted. Miles evaded the issue and wrote wordy dispatches that said little. After a month of voluminous correspondence, the President decided that the terms were such that the prisoners could not honorably be turned over to the civil authorities. He therefore directed that they resume the journey to Florida.[18]

17. Gatewood, "Surrender of Geronimo," pp. 34-44. Lawton's report in Secretary of War, *Annual Report* (1886), pp. 176-81. Wood in Miles, *Personal Recollections*, pp. 506-17. Miles in ibid., pp. 519-25. Official correspondence covering the period of Miles' command is published in House Executive Documents, 49th Cong., 2d sess., No. 117.

18. Secretary of War, *Annual Report* (1886), pp. 12-15, 144-46. Miles contended that a misunderstanding had arisen through the failure of General Howard, his immediate superior as division commander in San Francisco, to relay the full report of the surrender, in which the terms were set forth. "One cause of the trouble," Miles wrote to his wife, "was that General Howard or some one at his headquarters suppressed my full account of the surrender of Geronimo, and sent a short dispatch of his own saying they had surrendered unconditionally." Virginia W. Johnson, *The Unregimented General: A Biography of Nelson A. Miles* (Boston, Houghton Mifflin, 1962), p. 253.

Many aspects of the Apache confinement in Florida aroused the indignation of organizations dedicated to defending Indian rights. They pointed out that Miles' action in taking the reservation Chiricahuas from their mountain homes to unhealthful captivity in Florida was bad enough. But to treat the men who had loyally served Crook as scouts in the same way was worse yet. Even Kayitah and Martine, who at Miles' behest had gone with Gatewood to persuade Geronimo to surrender, had been sent to Florida. Miles had promised Geronimo and Natchez that they would be sent out of the Southwest *with their families.* Yet the men were confined at Fort Pickens and the women and children at Fort Marion. Finally, removed from their natural habitat, the Apaches began to die in alarming numbers.

In Generals Crook and Oliver O. Howard the friends of the Indian found powerful allies. Crook made speeches, wrote pamphlets, and talked with congressmen and senators in an attempt to dramatize the plight of the Chiricahuas and the injustice done them. The campaign aroused heated opposition from General Miles and his supporters, and a violent controversy raged that abated only slightly when Crook died in 1890. Nevertheless, largely as a result of the activities of Crook, Howard, and the Indian Rights Association, the men at Fort Pickens were united with their families in 1887. A year later they were sent to Mount Vernon Barracks, Alabama, and joined the rest of the Chiricahuas, who had already been moved to this more healthful location. At last, in 1894, the entire tribe was moved, over the vigorous objection of Miles and the western press, to Fort Sill, Oklahoma. Here Geronimo died on February 17, 1909. In 1913, 187 Chiricahuas were permitted to transfer to the Mescalero Apache Reservation in New Mexico. The rest chose to remain at Fort Sill, where the remnant of the tribe lives today.[19]

19. A good résumé of the controversy is given in Schmitt, pp. 289-300. The complete details of the dispute, together with pertinent correspondence covering the surrender, were published in House Executive Documents, 49th Cong., 2d sess., No. 117. See also Herbert Welsh, *The Apache Prisoners at Fort Marion, St. Augustine, Florida* (Indian Rights Association, 1887). Commissioner of Indian Affairs, *Annual Report* (1913), p. 34; (1914), pp. 56-57.

Miles rose to command the United States Army. As he advanced, so too did Lawton and Wood, both of whom possessed unquestioned abilities. But by contrast, Gatewood sank to obscurity. His health broken by the rigors of the Sierra Madre, and injured in a dynamite explosion, he was retired a first lieutenant and died at an early age.

After resigning from the Army in 1886, Britton Davis became superintendent of the Corralitos Mining and Cattle Company, the property of a New York firm on the eastern flank of the Sierra Madre in Chihuahua. Except for brief service as a major in the Spanish-American War, he devoted most of his subsequent career to this enterprise. The business collapsed in the political chaos that followed the fall of Mexican President Porfirio Diaz in 1911. Davis then made his home in Congers, New York, and after serving as a "dollar a year man" in Washington during World War I, he moved to San Diego, California, in 1924 to live in retirement. Here he wrote *The Truth about Geronimo*.[20]

In an interview with a newsman, Davis explained why he had written the book and why he called it *The Truth about Geronimo:* "I got dadblamed [this was not his real adjective, said the reporter] tired of hearing so many untruths about Geronimo and his capture that I sat down and wrote the truth about it. Geronimo was never captured."[21] Too, part of Davis' motivation sprang from a controversy he had been carrying on for several years in veterans' circles with Gen. James Parker, another participant in the Geronimo campaign and an admirer of General

20. *Dallas Morning News,* March 30, 1930. Obituary by Col. Charles B. Gatewood in *Annual Report of the Association of Graduates of the United States Military Academy at West Point, New York,* June 11, 1930, pp. 157-59.

21. *San Diego Sun,* Oct. 25, 1929. This was not entirely true, asserted the mercurial Apache agent John Clum. He himself had actually seized Geronimo and put him in chains at the Warm Springs Agency, New Mexico, in 1877, before Geronimo's name became a household word in the nation. On every subsequent occasion, as Clum points out, Geronimo was not captured but was induced to surrender. See John P. Clum, *Victorio, Chief of the Warm Springs Apaches in 1877, at Ojo Caliente, New Mexico,* reprint from *New Mexico Historical Review* (Santa Fe, 1929).

Miles. Davis' book was published in October 1929, only a few months after Parker's memoirs were released.[22]

Britton Davis died on January 23, 1930, three months after the publication of his book. But history has profited from the controversy in which he and his contemporaries engaged, for Geronimo's downfall, an event of enormous significance in the history of the Southwest, can now be viewed in its true light. Gatewood it was indeed who entered the camp of Geronimo at great personal risk and alone persuaded him to give up. But Crawford and Wirt Davis, with Crook behind them, and then Lawton, Wood, and the regulars, with Miles behind them, so harried the Apache hostiles that Gatewood was enabled to succeed. The tragedy—and the origins of the controversy—lay in Gatewood's shoddy reward and in the unjust treatment of Crook's loyal Apache scouts who had contributed so importantly to the final outcome.

22. *Dallas Morning News,* March 10, 1930. James Parker, *The Old Army Memories, 1872-1918* (Philadelphia, Dorrance, 1929).

Contents

List of Illustrations

Author's Preface

THE Geronimo campaign of 1885-86, against the Apache Indians of the Southwest, was in some respects one of the most remarkable in recorded history. The whole of it has never been, will never be told. It is my task to throw some light upon the causes leading to the outbreak of May 17, 1885, and to describe briefly the baleful results and the extraordinary contest that followed.

In this campaign thirty-five men and eight half-grown or older boys, encumbered with the care and sustenance of 101 women and children, with no base of supplies and no means of waging war or of obtaining food or transportation other than what they could take from their enemies, maintained themselves for eighteen months, in a country two hundred by four hundred miles in extent, against five thousand troops, regulars and irregulars, five hundred Indian auxiliaries of these troops, and an unknown number of civilians.

During that time they killed seventy-five citizens of Arizona and New Mexico of whom we have official records; twelve friendly White Mountain Apache near Fort Apache; two commissioned officers and eight soldiers of our regular army, and an unknown number, probably a hundred or more, Mexicans or others not of record.

Their losses in killed were six men, two large boys, two women and one child, *not one of whom was killed by regular troops*. Moreover, one of the boys and two of the men were not killed in open warfare, but were killed by the citizens of the town of Casas Grandes, Chihuahua, where they had gone on a peace mission.

When Geronimo surrendered to Miles, two men, two women, a girl, and a small boy slipped away and returned to Mexico. They were subsequently killed, one or two at a time, by the Mexicans.

Forty-three men and boys capable of bearing arms left the Reservation. Ten were killed as above stated. The Secretary of War in his annual report for 1886 says that at Fort Marion there were incarcerated sixteen men and large boys of Chihuahua's party; at Fort Pickens fifteen of Geronimo's and two of Mangus'; a total of thirty-three.

So much fiction has been written of the Apache by persons whose knowledge of them was gained from barroom talk, and so many self-glorifiers have claimed a part in the *capture* of Geronimo, who was never *captured* by anyone, that I feel the necessity for authenticating my connection with the Apache of the San Carlos Reservation, especially with the Chiricahua band to which Geronimo belonged, by the following extracts:

Records of the Adjutant General's Office, Washington, D. C.

On duty with troop L, Third Cavalry, at Fort D. A. Russell, Wyoming, to May 30, 1882. En route to and on duty at Fort Thomas, Arizona, to September 28, 1882. Commanding Companies B and E, Indian Scouts, and Acting Assistant Quartermaster and Assistant Chief of Staff at San Carlos, Arizona, to May 21, 1884. (In the field on detached service at San Bernardino, Arizona, December 20, 1883, to March 16, 1884.) Commanding Company B, Indian Scouts, at Turkey Creek, Arizona, to November, 1884. Near Fort Apache to May, 1885. In the field to September, 1885. On leave of absence to June 1, 1886. Resigned.

From the report for 1884 of Brigadier General George Crook, U.S. Army, commanding the Department of Arizona.

The Chiricahuas were then allowed to choose any part of the Reservation upon which to live, and, having selected a camp on Turkey Creek in the northern part of it they . . . 520 men, women, and children—were moved to that place in May, in which vicinity they are at present under the charge of Lieutenant Britton Davis, Third Cavalry.

The present contentment and quietness of the Chiricahua Indians is due greatly to the intelligence, patience, and firmness of Lieutenant Britton Davis, Third Cavalry, immediately under whose care they have been since they camped on Turkey Creek.

I am on the pension rolls of the Government for services rendered in the Geronimo Campaign of 1885-86. Crook, Crawford, and Gatewood have "crossed the cañon"; and, I trust, are waiting for me on the other side.

In relating my experiences with the Apache it will be my purpose to stick to facts; otherwise this narrative, lacking the historical feature I design for it, would have little value. If minor inaccuracies creep in they must be attributed to lapse of time and a faulty memory. No effort at romantic embellishment or poetic description will be made. Strict chronological sequence for incidents will not be adhered to unless the incidents have a bearing on what is to follow or what has gone before.

I deplore the use of the designations "buck" and "squaw" for the men and women of our North American Indians, a race of fellow human beings whose many fine qualities we have been too prone to becloud under hate and misunderstanding. The designations will not be used again in this narrative.

B. D.

San Diego, California
June, 1929.

Introduction

THE origin of the name "Apache" is not positively known. These Indians themselves had no generic name for the entire Apache people. Some authorities give the names of "Tinneh," "Dinde," "Yndye," etc.; but Navaho to whom I talked denied that any such appellations applied to them. As far as I was able to get at the truth, different tribes had different names, but no general name for the entire people who spoke the Apache dialect. The Apache of San Carlos claimed that the name "Apache" had been given them by the Mexicans; and they resented its use, claiming that it was a bad word, an affront.

It is quite possible that the word is of Spanish derivation. The early Spaniards had a custom of giving names of their own invention to tribes of marked characteristics—Chiricahua, chatterer, from their incessant yelling and chattering when making an attack—Tonto, foolish, to a tribe that spoke both the Apache and Mohave languages and understood either or neither as best suited their convenience.

The Apache had a distinct method of torture for the wounded who fell into their hands. They were turned over to the women and children who amused themselves by crushing the bones of the unfortunates with rocks. There is an old Spanish word, *apachurar,* meaning "to crush." *Apachureros de huesos*—"Crushers of bones"—shortened by time and use to "Apaches"? Well, the guess is as good as any other.

Who are the Apache? Unquestionably the descendants of migratory Mongol (Tartar) tribes of northern

Asia who had crossed over to the American continent at Behring Strait and made their way south, or were driven south by other migratory peoples who followed them—Ute, Wichita, Comanche, etc.[1] Bourke, Schwatka, and other investigators have traced them back to a kinship with certain Eskimo tribes in the Arctic. When civilization first came in contact with them four hundred years ago they were nomads; and nomads they remained until our little regular army at the end of the Civil War began driving them into the reservations the Government set aside for them—a process that took twenty years.

The Spaniards first met with them on Coronado's expedition of 1541 through southern Arizona, New Mexico, and western Texas. A. F. Bandelier, one of the most exact and conscientious of our investigators of the prehistoric peoples of the Southwest, thus describes Coronado's meeting with them:

> The troop came upon the first Indians of the plains about seventeen days after leaving Pecos. Coronado pertinently designates these people as those "who go around the country with the cows." The Prairie Indian, who lives on the bison, also, as it were, lives with him. These aborigines dwelt in tents of buffalo hide; they had no agriculture; they dressed in buffalo skins, and kept dogs, which they used as beasts of burden. The Spanish writers call them Querechos. There is no doubt that they were Apaches, and of the group which were called Vaqueros in the beginning of the sixteenth century, because they were associated exclusively with the "wild cow" (or bison). This tribe used the dog as a pack and draft animal as late as the middle of the last century. The species apparently belongs to the family of the Arctic dog, and probably came down with the Apaches from the north. I do not know whence the name of

[1] There is no consensus of scholarly opinion upon the question of the place of origin of the American Indians. Editor.

"Querechos" is derived, unless it is a pueblo name from the Jemez dialect, which was spoken in Pecos. It has some resemblance to "Oi-ra-uash," by which the Queres Indians designated a savage tribe that threatened the pueblos from the plains previous to the arrival of the Spaniards.

The Querecho, or Apache, as I shall hereafter call them, were friendly toward the Spaniards; but they knew nothing of Quivira and its treasures.[1]

Evidently at that time there were no Apache in southern Arizona or southern New Mexico, the inhabitants of those sections being a peaceful people occupying permanent villages. Sixty years later, in 1598, we find Oñate, the conqueror and pacifier of New Mexico, assigning to Father Francisco de San Miguel for conversion to Christianity among others the Pecos Indians "and those who have buffalo, as far as the Sierra Nevada; to Father Francisco de Zamora the Picuris and the *Apache* to the north and west of the Sierra Nevada, and the Taos," etc. Doubtless the Apache here referred to were the Navaho in northeastern Arizona and northwestern New Mexico —too far north for Coronado to meet them.

The Apache, even as late as the end of the eighteenth century, were a numerous and powerful nation. They roamed over all the country from the Arizona-New Mexico border on the west to San Antonio, Texas, on the east. To the north, they followed the buffalo into Kansas, Nebraska, and southern Wyoming. To the south, they were a terror to the colonists of the present Mexican states of Coahuila, Nuevo León, and eastern Chihuahua.

Their power in central and western Texas was finally

[1] From *The Gilded Man* (New York, 1893), pp. 225-226, by permission of D. Appleton & Company, publishers.

weakened by the Spaniards, who incited strife between the various tribes. What the Spaniards began the Comanche finished. These warriors, bitter enemies of the Apache, were also nomads, fully as warlike, even more ferocious, and better fighters. Gradually they drove the Apache from the plains of Texas and they fell back to the mountains of the West. As late as 1874, however, there were remnants of them still in western Texas, for we find them forming a part of Quana Parker's seven hundred warriors in the fight on the Canadian at Adobe Walls.[1]

Wars with the whites, with other Indian tribes, and among themselves, and the ravages of disease, principally epidemics of measles and smallpox, had by 1881 reduced this once great nation to less than thirty thousand souls, who almost without exception had accepted the inevitable and were living peaceably on the reservations in Arizona and New Mexico that had been set aside for them by the Government.

The Indians of the White Mountain Reservation, however, were in a state of unrest; individual bands were leaving the Reservation from time to time and committing depredations on neighboring ranches and settlements. One band of about 150 were openly at war with both the Americans and the Mexicans, not excepting at times certain of the Apache tribes who had incurred their displeasure.

This band had taken refuge in the Sierra Madre Mountains of Mexico, on the border of the states of Sonora and Chihuahua, where they defied the efforts of

[1] Adobe Walls was a small trading center established in 1874 in modern Hutchinson County, Texas. The Indian attack alluded to in the text occurred on June 27, 1874. Editor.

the Mexicans to exterminate them. They were constantly raiding the Mexican settlements in western Chihuahua and eastern Sonora, occasionally extending their pillaging operations north into Arizona and New Mexico, and returning to the fastnesses of the Sierra Madre Mountains when pursued by American troops. There they were safe from pursuit, as our troops were not permitted to enter Mexico.

The Indians of this band were principally of the Chiricahua tribe with a part of the Warm Springs, a few Coyotero, and some renegades from other bands of the White Mountain Reservation.

In the latter part of August, 1881, a medicine man of the White Mountain tribe living near Fort Apache stirred up the Indians of that vicinity by incantations and incitements to war. An attempt to arrest him resulted in a mutiny of some of the Indian scouts on August 30, 1881, who joined forces with a small contingent of malcontents. Captain Hentig of the Sixth Cavalry and several of his men were killed. The hostiles, some fifty or sixty in number, scattered in the mountains, where they remained a constant menace to settlers near the borders of the Reservation and a nucleus that harbored other renegades, criminals, and malcontents. When pursued they scattered or took refuge among the peaceable Indians, who fed and protected them. The efforts of the military to subdue them were paralyzed by the opposition of the Interior Department at Washington, under whose charge all the Indians were.

At this time there were about six thousand Apache on the White Mountain Reservation, the headquarters of the Agency being at San Carlos in the junction of the San Carlos and Gila rivers. About twenty-five miles up the Gila from San Carlos, at the abandoned military post of Camp Goodwin, a subagency had been established for those Indians of the Chiricahua and Warm Spring bands who had made peace and were living there under their principal chiefs, Loco, Nana, and Juh. They were about 375 in number, nearly all of them Warm Springs and Chiricahua. Geronimo, who attained prominence later, was among them.

Several of the Chiricahua were present at the Cibicu when Hentig was killed, on August 30. About a month later the Chiricahua at Camp Goodwin under Juh and Geronimo killed the agency chief of police, Sterling, attempted to kill the subagent, Hoag, and started for Mexico. Near Fort Grant two troops of the Sixth Cavalry intercepted them and lost a sergeant and three men killed. The Indians thereafter avoided contact with the troops and got safely to Mexico.

Loco and Nana with their Warm Springs, about 150 in number, refused at that time to join in the outbreak and remained quietly at the subagency.

The Apache of the White Mountain Reservation were not the only Apache in Arizona and New Mexico. There were some twenty thousand Navaho on the Navaho Reservation in northeastern Arizona and about two thousand Mescalero on their reservation in eastern New Mexico. But these tribes were peaceable and gave no trouble. Some Mescalero enlisted as scouts in the Geronimo campaign of 1885-86.

Chapter I

I report for duty in Wyoming. Loco's outbreak. Third Cavalry ordered to Arizona. White Mountain kill Colvig. Pursuit by troops.

ON December 1, 1881, I reported for duty at Fort D. A. Russell, Wyoming, as Second Lieutenant, Troop L, Third Cavalry, to which I had been assigned after graduating from the Military Academy the previous summer.

In May, 1882, a war party of Chiricahua came up from Mexico to the Camp Goodwin subagency and forced the Indians there under Loco to return with them to Mexico. Their trek south was marked with the usual slaughter of everything human in their way. Troops from the posts in southern Arizona and New Mexico were sent in pursuit of them and had one or two skirmishes with their rear guard. But the Indians were well mounted and moved with such rapidity that they escaped to Mexico with little loss of their effective fighting men.

Just below the international border a force of Mexican troops intercepted them by accident, the troops being on the march from a station in Chihuahua to another in Sonora. The Indian warriors were a couple of miles in the rear of the main body of women, children, and old men, watching some of our troops who were pursuing them. The women and children ran into the Mexican trap and were being slaughtered when the warriors, hearing the firing, raced up and made it so hot for the Mexicans that many of the women and children escaped;

but they left many dead on the field. One old Indian, however, took heavy toll of the Mexicans. Concealed in a small depression in the ground, behind a clump of cacti, he killed eight Mexican soldiers before his ammunition gave out and they were able to get him.

The accretion of Loco's people swelled the number of hostiles in Mexico to over four hundred, nearly a third of them men and boys able to bear arms. The menace to the settlers in Arizona and New Mexico was increased. Moreover, the Indians remaining on the Reservation were in a state of bitter resentment over the treatment they were receiving at the hands of the civilians in charge of them. Unless controlled and better treated, other outbreaks were sure to follow.

The Third Cavalry had had experience in fighting Apache ten years previously under General George Crook. It was still serving under him in the Department of the Platte. The War Department decided to send Crook back to Arizona and the Third Cavalry was ordered there at once. Troop L was assigned to Fort Thomas, on the Gila River at the southeastern edge of the White Mountain Reservation and about twenty-eight miles above the Agency at San Carlos.

The only officer's family accompanying the troops assigned to Fort Thomas was the wife and four children of Lieutenant Morton. The sudden change from the climate of Wyoming to the bottom lands of the Gila, with a temperature of 110° in the shade on their arrival there, was too much for them. They became ill and it was necessary to send them to a climate where they could recover.

Morton requested that I accompany him and the family to the railroad as some little added help in case they were attacked by one of the small bands of hostiles that were constantly leaving the Reservation for raids through the surrounding country. We made the forty-seven miles to Camp Grant at night in a government ambulance and stopped there in the morning to rest Mrs. Morton and the children, intending to go on to the railroad station at Willcox in the afternoon.

Colonel Shafter of the First Infantry was in command at Camp Grant. As we were preparing to leave, the Colonel's orderly came running to us with orders from the Colonel to report to him at once. Shafter had just received a telegram from our Colonel, Brackett, at Fort Thomas. Another Indian outbreak had occurred, our troops had taken the field, and we were ordered to join them at once. Mrs. Morton and the children were sent on to the railroad with a couple of infantrymen as guards.

There was a stage line that carried the mail from Willcox to Camp Grant, Fort Thomas, and Maxey, a small town near Fort Thomas. It came through Camp Grant about five o'clock that afternoon and Morton and I took it.

At Fort Thomas, the next morning, we found that twelve men had been left as escort for us through the Reservation, the report at Fort Thomas being that the outbreak had occurred at the Agency and that the hostiles had gone north with the troops in pursuit. By two days of hard riding we overtook the troops at the Salt River crossing of the old Apache-Navaho trail and learned from the officers with the command what had happened.

Two days before, about ten o'clock in the morning of July 17, a party of fifty-four White Mountain from near Fort Apache had descended upon the San Carlos Agency and killed Colvig, successor to Sterling as chief of the agency police, and seven of his Indian police. They had then started on a raid north through the San Carlos Valley, passed a little to the east of Globe, changed direction to northwest and crossed the Salt River at the mouth of Tonto Creek, where the Roosevelt Dam is now located.

These Indians were the hostile band of White Mountain and mutinous scouts who had killed Captain Hentig and his men the previous autumn at Cibicu Creek. The hostiles, we learned later, had brought no women with them from Fort Apache, but on leaving San Carlos after killing Colvig had forced five of the San Carlos Indian women to accompany them, one with a six-months-old baby in her arms.

Also, Morton and I learned why we had been honored with an escort of about a dozen armed Apache who had joined us as we were leaving San Carlos. The leader of the escort was a prominent White Mountain chief known as Sanchez. When the hostiles decided to raid San Carlos they stole a number of Indian ponies from the peaceful Indians at Fort Apache. But they made the mistake of stealing a pony that was the apple of Sanchez' eye. So he had gone on the warpath himself and with a dozen of his braves had followed the hostiles to San Carlos. Meeting Morton and me with our dozen troopers, he had decided to "throw in" with us, but for lack of an interpreter had been unable to explain his coöperation.

With our Fort Thomas command of four troops of the Third Cavalry, about 150 men, were Captains Drew, Vroom, and Crawford, and Lieutenants Morton, Porter, Boughton, West, and Davis. Drew, as senior captain, was in command. A pack train of about thirty packs had accompanied the command from Fort Thomas. The mules were in poor condition and the packers were having trouble keeping them up with the command.

I was detailed to see that they did keep up, but that night Drew decided on a night march. The trail led through a creek bottom with reeds and underbrush higher than the mules' heads. The bell had been taken off the bell horse for fear of alarming the hostiles. Fifteen minutes after we got into the creek bottom you could not have heard the bells of Saint Paul's Cathedral. It seemed to me that there were mules scattered all over central Arizona. They were all lost, wanted to get back to the bell horse, and determined that I should know it if their voices held out.

That night I completed my education in pack train profanity. What those packers said in English, Spanish, Indian, Irish, and German left nothing more to be desired. We overtook the command about ten o'clock the next morning but had to leave two packers still hunting for lost mules. The troops had fared little better; men and horses were exhausted and that attempt at a night march had gained us only about ten miles. It cost us all chance we had of getting into the fight.

Our command was not the only one in the field, and the movements of the others were of far more importance. For information as to these I am indebted to General Thomas Cruse, Colonel George L. Converse, and Colonel George H. Morgan, all at that time second lieutenants of cavalry.

At the same time that our command left Fort Thomas

two troops of the Third Cavalry under Captains Russel and Wessels and two of the Sixth Cavalry under Captains Chaffee and Wallace, with eight Tonto Indian scouts under Lieutenant Morgan with Al Sieber as chief of scouts, left Whipple Barracks and made Verde, forty-two miles, that day. By forced marching they reached Wild Rye on Tonto Creek two days later. Shortly after camping for the night one of the Bixby brothers, who had a large ranch in Tonto Basin, rode into camp, wounded, and reported that their ranch had been burned and his brother killed.

Chaffee with his company and the scouts under Sieber immediately broke camp and started for Tonto Basin, leaving the rest of the command to follow. Morgan remained back to bring a pack train from Verde through Hardscrabble Cañon. This accomplished, he cut across country alone and overtook Chaffee just before the fight began.

Two troops of the Sixth Cavalry under Kramer and Abbott with Lieutenants Cruse and Hodgson; two troops of the Third Cavalry under Lieutenants Converse, Hardie, and Johnson, and four White Mountain Apache scouts under Lieutenant Dodd, all under command of Major Evans, Third Cavalry, had left Fort Apache the morning of the eleventh and cut the hostile trail at the Salt River crossing a little ahead of our Fort Thomas command.

One troop of the Third under Lieutenant Chase and one troop of the Sixth under Lieutenant Kingsbury from Verde had taken the old Crook trail around the escarpment of Tonto Basin to cut the trail to the Navaho country should the hostiles head that way—which they did; but Chase and Kingsbury were a few hours too late to get into the fight.

Thus within three or four hours of the outbreak, fourteen troops of cavalry were in pursuit of the hostiles under orders so well planned that five troops were in the fight and six more less than ten miles away when the fight occurred. I have gone somewhat into detail in the matter of troop movements as it is typical of what occurred whenever there was an Indian outbreak—Apache, Sioux, Comanche, Modoc, or whatever turbulent tribe essayed to leave the reservation set aside for them.

I may add, however, that this was the only effective concentration of troops ever made against the Apache; and had the Apache been led by such captains as Victorio, Cochise, Mangus Colorado, Nana, or even Geronimo, the concentration would not have been effective. Such a leader would have known the number of troops near him and the Indians would not have stopped to give battle to Chaffee. They would have scattered in the mountains like quail when the hawk dives. But their leader, a White Mountain known as Na-ti-o-tish, lacked experience, or was not "gifted with the capacity of taking infinite pains." He made a mistake that was fatal to him and to nearly all of his men.

Chaffee cut the trail of the hostiles in Tonto Basin just ahead of the troops from Fort Apache under Evans. A patrol from Evans overtook Chaffee and established communication, advising Chaffee that help was near if needed.

The night of the sixteenth Chaffee sent word back to Evans that he was close on the hostiles and needed reinforcements. Troop E of the Third Cavalry under Converse was the lead troop on the march with Evans' command and was rushed ahead, joining Chaffee the morning of the seventeenth, the other troops of that command following close behind.

And here the hostiles made their fatal mistake. Chaffee's troop was a white-horse troop. So was E Troop under Converse. The Indians were watching Chaffee. They knew to a man the strength of his troop, as they had been watching him the day before. If they saw Converse's troop of white horses at all, they mistook them for stragglers from Chaffee's. And they failed to ascertain that close behind Converse were three more troops of cavalry. So they decided to lead Chaffee into a trap and massacre his command, which they knew they outnumbered.

Another thing the hostiles failed to note was that Chaffee had been joined by the Tonto scouts from McDowell and the White Mountain scouts from Fort Apache. These scouts, under Morgan and Sieber, detected the hostiles' trap and saved Chaffee from walking into it.

The trap was very ingeniously laid. The trail led down into a cañon, a volcanic crack in the earth over a thousand feet deep with almost perpendicular sides. From top to top it was about seven hundred yards across, with a stream of crystal clear water at the bottom. The cañon was known to us as Chevelon's Fork of the Cañon Diablo; but for some reason it is called Big Dry Wash in the army records of the fight. Some idea of the difficulty of crossing it may be gained from the fact that it took me, the day after the fight, three-quarters of an hour to go from the position of our troops on the one side to the position of the Indians on the other. And no one was shooting at me.

The hostiles, with their plunder from the ranches they had raided and the horses they had stolen, had crossed the cañon, ascended the opposite side to near the top, and sent their horses back out of sight on the level ground at the top of the cañon. Building skilfully concealed parapets of loose rocks, they waited for what they supposed was only Chaffee's troop to get down into the cañon, where they would probably have been wiped out to a man. The hostiles outnumbered Chaffee's troop, and were as well or better armed and well fortified; while the soldiers, scattered along the trail in the open, would have been easy targets.

But the keen eyes of the Indian scouts with Morgan and Sieber detected the ambush. Chaffee and Converse halted on the edge of the cañon; the remainder of Evans' command, three more troops, came up, and the ball opened.

Chapter II

The fight at Chevelon's Fork (Big Dry Wash). The wounded girl. "Arrest no Indians."

FOR the following description of the fight, the most successful our troops ever had with the Apache after they had obtained modern arms, I am indebted to General, then Lieutenant, Thomas Cruse, U.S. Army, Retired, whose gallantry in this action won him the Congressional Medal of Honor. And it is a safe bet that he is prouder of it than he is of the star of a brigadier general which now adorns his uniform when he has occasion to wear it.

The hostiles had seen Chaffee's troop, which was mounted on white horses, and had kept it under observation from about three o'clock until dark, had counted his men and concluded to ambush him the next day under circumstances favorable to themselves. But they had not seen the Fort Apache column at all, and their watchers reported the next morning that Chaffee's troop was still alone.

Colonel Evans told Chaffee to keep ahead the next morning as if he were acting alone and we would follow at daybreak. Troop I, Converse, Third Cavalry, also on white horses, would be in the lead at the head of our column, so that if the Indians did stop to fight Chaffee, he would have two troops on white horses to engage them at once and the other troops could be placed to the best advantage as they came up.

At daylight on July 17 we moved out cautiously and

saw Chaffee climb the rim of the basin unopposed; then we followed, reached General Springs and saw signs of the hostile camp of the night before; then on, cursing our luck over the prospect of a tedious campaign in the rough, waterless Navaho country. About a mile farther, a mounted courier from Chaffee dashed up. Converse with his white-horse troop rushed forward at a gallop, and word was passed along that the Indians were camped on the far side of a deep crack in the earth, a branch of Cañon Diablo (Big Dry Wash) with all arrangements to give Chaffee the fight of his life. The location was about three miles from where we were, and as we rapidly approached we could hear casual shots and an occasional volley crash.

When Sieber and the scouts located the hostiles on the far side of the chasm, Chaffee dismounted his troop and sent a few men forward to the brink. When these were seen the hostiles opened fire; then Converse galloped up, dismounted almost in plain view of the hostiles, sent his horses to the rear and advanced in line of skirmishers along the edge of the cañon as if intending to go down the trail. Both troops and hostiles then opened up a heavy fire across the cañon.

The scene of action was in a heavy pine forest, thickly set with large pine trees (park-like, with no underbrush or shrubbery whatever) on a high mesa at the summit of the Mogollon Range. Across this mesa from east to west ran a gigantic slash in the face of the earth, a volcanic crack, some seven hundred yards across and about one thousand feet deep, with almost perpendicular walls for miles on either side of the very steep trail which led to the Navaho country. This crossing point was held by the hostiles and their fire covered every foot of the trail, descending and ascending.

When Colonel Evans and his troops rode up and quickly dismounted about three hundred yards from the brink of the cañon, Chaffee reported to him, outlined the situation, and started to suggest some dispositions of the troops. Evans stopped him; told him to dispose of the troops as he saw best, and gave him full control, saying that he, Chaffee, had located the Indians and it was his fight.

This was one of the most unselfish actions of relinquishing command that ever came to my notice during a long career in the army; because, mind you, Chaffee was not only Evans' junior (a captain) but also belonged to another cavalry regiment, the Sixth; while Colonel Evans belonged to the Third, and there is always rivalry for honors between regiments so thrown together.

Chaffee got busy at once; ordered Kramer and Cruse with Troop E, Sixth Cavalry, his (Chaffee's) own troop, I, Sixth Cavalry, commanded by Lieutenant Frank West, and part of the Indian scouts under Sieber to go cautiously to the right of the trail and cross where possible about a mile to the east. When the far side of the cañon had been gained, they were to form for attack and close in on the main trail. Converse and his troop were told to keep up a heavy fire across the chasm. Troop K, Sixth Cavalry, Captain L. A. Abbott and Lieutenant F. G. Hodgson; Troop E, Third Cavalry, Lieutenants F. H. Hardie and F. C. (Friday) Johnson, and the remainder of the Indian scouts under Lieutenant George H. Morgan, Third Cavalry, were sent to cross the cañon to the west and then move east.

A small guard from each troop was left with the pack trains and led horses to protect them from surprise should any of the hostiles succeed in gaining our side of the cañon unperceived.

These movements began about three o'clock in the afternoon and the sun was shining brightly. As we moved out, we heard that Converse had been shot in the head and was being brought in. I saw him as we passed and rushed up for a second and spoke to him. He said something was the matter with his eye but thought it would soon pass.

Poor fellow, it has never passed. A 44-caliber bullet had struck a piece of lava rock, split in two and one-half had penetrated the eye, wedging itself firmly in the eye socket where, in spite of the ministrations of the most noted surgeons of the world, it has remained ever since. He is still living, a colonel on the retired list after a most useful life to the Government, punctured at periods by almost unbearable pain from that wound.

Our column finally found a place where we could climb down the precipitous side of the chasm and had gained the beautiful stream that flowed at the bottom when someone exclaimed and pointed up,—every star was plainly visible in the sky at three-thirty in the after-noon.

By dint of strenuous climbing we finally reached the crest on the other side, formed skirmish line, I Troop on the right with Sieber and his scouts, and moved rapidly forward. Just as we started we heard the crash of several volleys and knew that the other encircling column was in action. Sieber and his Indians with I Troop ran into the Indian herd just then and as the hostile herd guard's attention had been attracted by the firing in the other direction, our people soon placed them *hors de combat.* The scouts rounded up the ponies, placed them behind our column with a guard, left them there, and moved on.

The other column, Abbott's, like ourselves finally negotiated the descent into the cañon and started up the other side. When almost at the top it ran into a party of Indians coming down a little side ravine with the evident intention of getting to the rear of what they supposed was Chaffee's white-horse troop still keeping up a fire from the edge of the cañon on the other side. As they thought there could be no opposition on their side they were proceeding rapidly and without the usual precautions when Abbott opened fire on them. Several were killed and wounded and all were thoroughly stampeded.

The fugitives, rushing back for their main camp and the pony herd, were joined by those of the camp who had been firing across the cañon. They were sure there was something wrong but could not tell what. As this main body of the hostiles came sweeping through the woods, we saw them and at first imagined they were trying to rush us and recapture the pony herd. But as a matter of fact they were totally unaware of our being there until we fired directly into them, causing further casualties, and drove them back.

West had swept the right of his line across the Navaho trail by this time so that line of retreat was cut off. We then swung our line in a semicircle toward the hostile camp, driving the hostiles in front of us and penning them against the edge of the cañon.

By this time, five o'clock, and the shadows heavy in the dense forest, I found myself in command of the left flank of Troop E, next to the brink of the cañon and probably two hundred yards in front of what had been the main camp of the hostiles, indicated only by some scattered blankets, cooking utensils, etc. Sieber was by my side.

As our line closed in there was a furious burst of fire from the hostiles, causing several casualties among the troops; among others Lieutenant Morgan, Third Cavalry, who had joined West after his Indian scouts had been left behind the line; and Sergeant Conn, Troop E, Sixth. As the line advanced from tree to tree, Morgan had chances to fire at hostiles several times and finally dropped one. Elated over his success he called out, "I got him." In doing this he exposed his position to another Indian in the same nest, who thereupon fired and got Morgan through the arm, into the side, and apparently through both lungs. The soldiers got the Indian.

We thought sure that Morgan would die that night but he is still living and in good health, a colonel on the retired list. The surgeon (Dr.—later Colonel—Ewing) found that when the bullet broke the arm bone its force was so lessened that it did not break the rib, as from the hole made we supposed it had, but slid around it under the skin and lodged in the muscles of the back, where it was dug out and presented to Morgan.

Sergeant Conn was a character in the Sixth Cavalry and had been with the regiment for about twenty years. In Arizona he had become well known to the Apache because of his issuing the rations when attached to the scout company. The Indians called him "Coche Sergeant" (hog or ration sergeant). He was a little dried-up Irishman with a terrible brogue, although claiming Boston as his birthplace.

When the line moved forward, Conn gave some orders to his men and immediately from the hostiles hidden in their nests (no other name for their protective works) arose the jeering yell, "Coche Sergeant! Coche Sergeant!" Conn answered them in kind and other kind, and one who could speak English invited him to come on down there and he would kill him. Conn again retorted and more vigorously, whereupon the Indian located him and fired. The bullet hit Conn full in the throat, made a ghastly hole, pushed aside the jugular vein (so the surgeon claimed), grazed the vertebra, and passed out, leaving a hole as big as a silver dollar; all this in a neck that wore a number thirteen collar.

Conn went down for the count in the midst of a thrilling repartee, and Captain Kramer standing about five feet away remarked to the First Sergeant, "I am afraid they got poor Conn." But Conn recovered and in telling the story used to say, "I heard the Captain say I was kilt, and I was not, only spacheless." The soldiers and Sieber got that bunch of Indians.

In the meantime I had pushed forward with Sieber, whom I saw kill three hostiles as they were creeping to the edge of the cañon to drop over. He would say, "There he goes!" then bang would go his rifle. The Indian that I had never seen, strain my eyes as I might, would, when hit, throw up his arms as if trying to seize some support, then under the impetus of his rush, plunge forward on his head and roll over several times. One, shot near the brink, plunged clear over and it seemed to me kept falling for ten minutes.

It was now about five-thirty and getting dusk; only about seventy-five yards and a little ravine some seven feet deep separated me and my men from the Indians in the camp. I knew that unless the camp was taken pretty quick the Indians would escape under cover of darkness, so I resolved to cross the ravine and take it. I told Sieber that I was going to do it, and much to my surprise he hastily remonstrated.

"Don't you do it, Lieutenant; don't you do it; there are lots of Indians over there, and they will get you sure."

"Why Al you have killed every one of them," I replied, and instructed my men what to do. They were to rush forward to the ravine, halt under cover, then, when ordered, were to advance at a run into the camp with some cartridges in the hand, guns loaded. We did just that and had no casualties; due, I think, to the fact that Captain Kramer's men and Sieber smothered the hostiles with their fire.

As we rushed forward on the other side of the ravine I soon discovered that, as Sieber had said, there were lots of Indians there, and we had business on our hands. But I had with me Sergeant Horan, Sergeant Martin, and six or eight other old timers that such things did not disconcert in the least, and things were going slap-bang when suddenly not over six feet away was an Indian with his gun leveled directly at me. It seemed he could not miss, so raising my gun, I stood awaiting the shock of the bullet. He was nervous and jerked the trigger sufficiently to barely miss me and hit a young Scotchman, McLellan, just to my left and probably a foot in the rear. McLellan fell; I fired and threw myself to the ground.

Sieber, Captain Kramer, and several others saw me go down and thought for sure I had been hit. I found I was not but saw McLellan lying almost beside me and asked if he was hit; he replied:

"Yes, Sir, through the arm; I think it is broken."

I told him to lie quietly and we would get back to the ravine. In a lull, I rose up and when I found he was unconscious, dragged him back about twenty feet where the slope protected us; rested a little, then back a little farther, and finally Sergeant Horan and myself got him to the bottom of the ravine.

In going back, as I rose up with McLellan, Abbott's men saw several hostiles rise up to fire, whom they had not seen before. Every man in the line turned loose on them, not knowing that I was in their direct line of fire at two hundred yards distance, and the way the air was filled with bullets showed that they were coming close inside their target. Several pieces of gravel and small fragments of rock or lead struck me in the face, making it bleed; I was sure that I was hit and would soon collapse. Kramer's men swarmed into the hostiles but darkness soon came on and the fight was over.

I grabbed some blankets from the Indian camp and made a nice bed for McLellan, but the bullet had smashed his rib and gone through both lungs. He quietly passed away about an hour later.

This ends Cruse's story. There were fifty-four hostiles in the fight. We subsequently learned that twenty-one were killed on the ground; five died later of their wounds; and not one escaped from the fight unwounded.

Shortly after our Fort Thomas command had camped the night of the seventeenth we had received a message from Evans telling us briefly of the engagement and ordering us to join him; this we did the following morning about eight o'clock, and I got my first demonstration of the courage and vitality of the Apache.

Lieutenant Hodgson had been left all night with a patrol on the side of the cañon the hostiles had occupied. During the night he heard groans and in the morning began, with his patrol, a cautious investigation to see if any wounded remained. Caution was necessary; a wounded Apache is as desperate and dangerous as a wounded wolf. Suddenly the men were fired on, a single shot evidently from a little parapet of loose rocks, from which powder smoke was rising, above them on the side of the cañon. The men took cover and opened fire on the parapet. A shot, and then another replied to them. The men continued their fire for a few minutes but getting no further action from the parapet, charged it.

Behind it they found a woman apparently eighteen or nineteen years of age, prone on the ground, shielding with her body a six-months-old baby. Drawing a knife from her girdle she fought the men until overpowered and disarmed. With her was a shriveled old hag of sixty or more who made no resistance. It was the younger woman who had used the rifle. Three cartridges were all she had and the empty shells lay beside her.

It was found at once that the young woman's leg had been broken by a bullet just above the knee. A makeshift stretcher of boughs was rigged up on the spot and she was brought over to our camp on the opposite side of the cañon; a task that, on account of the rugged and almost perpendicular sides of the cañon took almost two hours. She must have suffered terribly but did not utter a groan.

Almost immediately after she reached our camp one of those sudden rain and hail storms set in and lasted some ten or fifteen minutes. We had but scant shelter for our own wounded and could not quickly improvise a shelter for this wounded girl. In a moment she and her baby were covered with hail and drenched to the skin with ice-cold water. Our surgeons were so busy with our own wounded that they could not give her any attention until the following day, then they decided to amputate her leg.

Not a drop of anesthetics was to be had. The scanty supply brought by our surgeons had been used entirely in caring for our own men. There was not even a little whiskey to deaden the pain. Yet she stood it without a murmur.

It had been my intention to watch the operation, thinking that I might have a similar job to perform myself some day. You never knew what emergency might arise in Indian campaigning, and doctors with Indian scouts were practically unknown until General Wood immortalized them. My intentions were doubtless laudable, but when I caught a glance from that young woman's eyes as she watched the doctors getting ready I suddenly decided to get my surgical training some other way.

The day following the operation we had to break camp. We saddled a quiet pack mule with a cavalry saddle, covered it with several folds of a pack-train blanket, lifted her on the mule, gave her her baby, and put the old woman at leading the mule. In this way she "marched" with us through the mountains for the week it took us to reach Fort Apache. Three or four months later I saw her at San Carlos running around with a homemade crutch, fat and happy.

When the hostiles had reached the Salt River crossing of the Apache trail they had sent some of their party down the river to raid ranches in the valley, the main body continuing along the trail north.

There was an organization of barroom Indian fighters in Globe who called themselves the "Globe Rangers." The day following the outbreak the Rangers took the field, well primed with the best brand of whiskey that the town afforded, and carrying an ample supply with them.

At Bixby's ranch in the Tonto Basin, which the main body of hostiles had raided just in advance of them, killing one of the Bixby brothers and wounding the other, the Rangers camped at night, turned their horses loose to graze, put a guard over them, and went inside the ranch house for a carouse and a poker game; after which they went to sleep.

The guard became tired of the monotony of guard duty and joined the hilarious party in the ranch house. The band of hostiles who had gone down the river to raid settlements and were returning to join the main band, passed by the ranch about daylight the next morning, saw the opportunity, and ran off their horses.

The morning after the fight at Chevelon's Fork two of these men appeared in our camp looking for their horse stock. They began claiming every good-looking horse in the herd that our troops had captured from the Indians. I was standing beside Chaffee who, with his hands in his pockets, was letting them go as far as they liked, but getting madder every second at their evident lying. Presently one of them claimed Chaffee's own saddle mare and his companion backed him up in the claim. Then the air around me took on a blue tinge as the two sneaked out of camp under Chaffee's barrage. They got no horses. A few minutes later the rightful owner of the horses they had been claiming, the wounded Bixby brother, came into camp and recovered his stock.

En route to Fort Apache I was given command of the Indian scouts attached to our battalion with instructions to keep a lookout for any other hostile bands, or for any remnant of the band that the troops had fought at Chevelon's Fork. We arrived at Fort Apache a little after noon. Half an hour or so after our arrival one of my scouts came to me and through the interpreter told me that five of the Indians who had been in the Chevelon's Fork fight, all wounded, were in a rancheria he pointed out in the valley about a mile above the Post and in plain view from it.

"Come," he said in broken English "we go catchum killum!" his eyes glittering at the thought.

I could do nothing without orders from my battalion commander, Captain Drew. Drew decided that he needed authority from the post commander, his superior. The post commander was wary. He had experienced the wrath of the Interior Department in previous conflicts of authority over Indian affairs and decided to put the question up to the department commander at Whipple. The department commander put it up to the division commander at San Francisco, who referred it to the War Department in Washington. They consulted the Interior Department. All this, of course, by telegraph. Late the following afternoon there came back through "the proper military *Channels*" this order:

"You will molest no Indians living at peace on the Reservation!"

I mention this as an instance of the many "red tape" difficulties under which we operated in our efforts to subdue the hostile tribes of the West.

Chapter III

Crook takes command. Crawford, Gatewood, and Davis ordered to San Carlos. Bedfellows. "Hell's Forty Acres." Condition of the Indians. The Agent. Sieber, MacIntosh, Bowman, and Mickey Free. Scout companies organized. Secret service scouts. Indians counted. Males tagged. Principal bands. Pack trains. Agency traders. Beef delivery. Hay and wood purchases. Indian school graduates. Trial by jury. Sieber's joke. Indian delegates to Washington. Coal claim solution. An inexplicable tragedy.

ON September 4, 1882, General Crook took command of the Department of Arizona. He had previously subdued the Apache, in 1871-73, and knew them better than any other man in high command in the army. Nor was this knowledge confined to the Apache alone. Following the Civil War, wherein he had attained the rank of major general, he had been continuously on duty in the West, most of this time engaged in subduing the hostile tribes who were opposing the advance of civilization: Sioux, Cheyenne, Blackfeet, Crow, Ute, knew him, feared him, and respected him. From all, he had drawn a full meed of information that gave him an understanding of the Indian's nature, his good points and bad, equaled by no other officer of any rank in our army. As Bourke often said of him, "He was more Indian than the Indians themselves."

Immediately after taking command of the Department, Crook went to Fort Apache to learn from the Indians there the condition of affairs from their point of view. He met the principal chiefs, heard their complaints, promised to do what he could to rectify unjust conditions, and told them what in return he expected of them in the essentials of living at peace and going to work with a view to becoming self-supporting.

Continuing on to the Agency at San Carlos the General there prepared for business. He had been given full disciplinary control of the Indians of the entire Reservation, their rationing alone remaining under the jurisdiction of the Agent, and this subject to supervision of the military.

The following officers had been ordered to report to the General at San Carlos:

Emmet Crawford, Captain, Third Cavalry; Charles B. Gatewood, First Lieutenant, Sixth Cavalry; and Britton Davis, Second Lieutenant, Third Cavalry. Later Hamilton Roach, Second Lieutenant, First Infantry, was ordered to report to Gatewood as his assistant at Fort Apache.

Our first night at San Carlos we slept on the ground without tents. When I started to roll up my bedding in the morning I found that I had had for a bedfellow a ten-inch centipede. I registered a complaint with Crawford but got scant sympathy.

"You were lucky," he said; "I found a young rattler in mine."

Another officer decided he had better examine his bed. Under the canvas in which we wrapped our blankets, he found a tarantula that could nearly have straddled an ordinary saucer. All that we lacked were a vinegarroon and a Gila monster to make our reptilian collection complete.

Fort Thomas was accredited the worst army post in the domains of Uncle Sam, and merited its reputation during the few months I spent there. But San Carlos won unanimously our designation of it as "Hell's Forty Acres."

A gravelly flat in the confluence of the two rivers rose some thirty feet or so above the river bottoms and was dotted here and there by the drab adobe buildings of the Agency. Scrawny, dejected lines of scattered cottonwoods, shrunken, almost leafless, marked the course of the streams. Rain was so infrequent that it took on the semblance of a phenomenon when it came at all. Almost continuously dry, hot, dust- and gravel-laden winds swept the plain, denuding it of every vestige of vegetation. In summer a temperature of 110° in the shade was cool weather. At all other times of the year flies, gnats, unnamable bugs,—and I was about to say "beasts of the air"—swarmed in millions. Curiously, in the worst heat of the summer most of the flies disappeared; left, evidently, for the mountain resorts.

Everywhere the naked, hungry, dirty, frightened little Indian children, darting behind bush or into wikiup at sight of you. Everywhere the sullen, stolid, hopeless, suspicious faces of the older Indians challenging you. You felt the challenge in your very marrow—that unspoken challenge to prove yourself anything else than one more liar and thief, differing but little from the procession of liars and thieves who had preceded you.

Crawford was born a thousand years too late. *Sans peur et sans reproche* would have been sung of him in ballads of the Middle Ages. Mentally, morally, and physically he would have been an ideal knight of King Arthur's Court. Six feet one, gray-eyed, untiring, he was an ideal cavalryman and devoted to his troop, as were the men of it to him.

He had a keen sense of humor but something had saddened his early life and I never knew him to laugh aloud. His respect for women amounted to veneration. Modest, self-effacing, kindly, he delighted in assigning to his subordinates opportunities and credit he might well have taken to himself,—a very rare trait in an officer of any army. His expressed wish was that he might die in the act of saving the lives of others. He got his wish, the only reward he ever received for as dangerous, arduous, and thankless a job as ever fell to any man.

Of us four, only Gatewood knew anything of the Apache. Graduated from West Point in 1877, his experiences with them began two years later in the fight with Victorio's band in the Black Range of New Mexico. Thereafter, until I met him, he was almost continuously engaged in campaigns and scouting expeditions against them. Tall, spare, of extraordinary endurance, patient and fearless, he was an ideal selection for the job of managing the White Mountain at Fort Apache. In the four years of Apache trouble that followed no man accomplished more, got less credit for it, or suffered such injustice as fell to his lot. I will have more to say of him later.

Of the five thousand Indians on the White Mountain Reservation about four thousand were at or near the Agency at San Carlos, depending for food on the government rations doled out to them there. Some two hundred of the chiefs and principal men assembled for a conference with the General. He heard their complaints, assured them he would have abuses corrected as far as possible for him to do so, and told them what he expected of those who wanted to live at peace and what the malcontents might expect of him if they "started anything."

The Indians had just cause for complaint. Some of the reservations originally assigned to them had been taken from them after they had established themselves there. Other reservations had been cut down and the hunting grounds, on which they depended for a large part of their sustenance, greatly restricted. They had been driven into this barren waste at San Carlos with no provision for their self-support. A nomad people who had lived off the country, subsisting on game, wild fruits, nuts, and certain herbs, they had not the faintest idea how to subsist by agriculture and no means to that end had they known how.

They did know, however, that rations provided for them by the Government were being openly sold to neighboring towns and mining camps. That beef on the hoof, forming the principal part of their rations, was so thin that it was hardly more than skin and bone. That the weekly issue of flour, the other principal portion of the ration, would hardly suffice a family for one day. That other components of the ration were almost negligible when issued and frequently not issued at all.

There is nothing equal to idleness as a breeder of discontent. Here were five thousand restless, nomadic people who all their lives had roamed unrestrained throughout the Southwest, with many generations of nomadic blood behind them, herded now into a small tract of desert land and told to sit down, fold their hands, and be "good Indian" no matter how much we lied to and robbed them. Eighty per cent of them, exclusive of the lucky thousand near Fort Apache, were living in the hot, barren, brush-covered bottom lands of the Gila and San Carlos rivers, within ten miles of the Agency established at the junction of the two rivers. Their principal occupation was gathering once a week at the Agency to receive the rations doled out to them. Is there any wonder that they were discontented?

The Bureau of Indian Affairs of the Department of the Interior at Washington had turned over to the army the task of controlling the Indians on the Reservation and of returning to the Reservation those still out; principally the Chiricahua and Warm Springs in Mexico. The Bureau, however, continued its Agent at the Agency to distribute the Indian rations.

The Agent when we took charge was a political appointee with a religious bent, as were about all the Indian agents of those days. A new appointee, he was outspoken in his detestation of his job and his contempt for the Indians. He had taken the position, he told us, only because of the salary when he could get nothing better; "and Arizona, a hole not fit for a dog, would see no more of him than would be absolutely necessary in order to hold the job." He was from Colorado and kept his word. He left shortly after we took charge and returned but once or twice, as far as I remember, during the following three years. His place was filled by his clerk, Colonel Beaumont, a fine old gentleman, an ex-officer of the Civil War, and an immediate buddy of ours. He gave every assistance and coöperation in his power, saw that the Indians got what was due them, and conducted his business in an irreproachable manner.

Crawford was placed in full military control of the entire Reservation with instructions from the General to report to him direct. To Gatewood was assigned the especial control of the White Mountain Apache with his station at Fort Apache. To me was assigned the command of the Apache scouts at San Carlos, the quartermaster and commissary duties at the post, and command at San Carlos in Crawford's absence. Our official designation was "on detached service as assistant chiefs of staff to the Commanding General of the Department."

For quarters Crawford and I, and one or two other officers who came to San Carlos later, were given a two-story adobe building about four hundred yards to the east of the main agency buildings. This building had been erected to house some school teachers from the East who had found the going too rough and had returned home after a very short effort at tutoring the Apache.

In addition to the building we occupied there was a large, one-story, adobe school building fifty or sixty feet to the west of, and three one-story adobe buildings to the east of, our quarters building, detached from, but forming with it a hollow square. The school building we used for meetings with the chiefs or principal men; for trials by jury when held; and for public functions generally. The three other buildings served for storerooms, messrooms, and quarters for civilian employees.

Al Sieber was appointed chief of scouts with Archie MacIntosh and Sam Bowman as his assistants. Mickey Free was enlisted as a scout with the pay of a first sergeant, but his rôle was that of interpreter. A short sketch of each of these men may be of interest.

Al Sieber, six feet one, about 190 pounds of bone and muscle, a little past forty years of age, was of Pennsylvania Dutch stock. He had been for eight years in the employ of the Government as scout and in various other capacities in operations against the Apache. Capable and courageous, the Indians feared and respected him. A better selection for chief of scouts could not have been made. True, he made a disastrous mistake in May, 1885, but we should remember him by the many critical situations he handled successfully over a period of nearly fifteen years, risking his life repeatedly that others might be saved. If there was ever a man who actually did not know physical fear, that man was Al Sieber! He was in no sense reckless, took all necessary precautions, but never hesitated when it became necessary to throw caution aside. He was in constant danger of assassination, as many of the Indians had personal grudges against him; but he went about his work as though all the world were his friends. Apache Kid finally shot him and caused him the loss of a leg, but this was after I left the service.

Archie MacIntosh had been a scout under the General in Arizona during his previous campaigns there. Originally he had come from the Hudson Bay country, but he had familiarized himself with the Apache during the ten years he had lived in Arizona. I will have occasion to mention him again.

Sam Bowman also had served under General Crook in earlier days. He was part Choctaw Indian, a faithful and courageous man. Later he was my interpreter at San Carlos and went with me to Turkey Creek in 1884 with the Chiricahua and Warm Springs.

Mickey Free, five feet five, slim but muscular, was the son of an Irish father and a Mexican mother. He had lost the sight of one eye which gave him a sinister appearance. Captured by the Apache when a small child, his life had been spent among them and he had become to all intents and purposes an Apache; was married to an Apache, dressed as an Apache, and lived as the scouts lived. He had retained, or acquired, a knowledge of Spanish, of which I also had a smattering, and became my interpreter during almost the entire time of my service. The Indians suspected him of coloring things to suit the whites; Sieber's opinion of him could not be printed in polite words. He may have fooled me on occasion, but if he did it was done so skilfully that I never found it out.

Several books and a number of magazine articles have come to my attention glorifying the deeds of various Apache chiefs of scouts, or other civilian subjugators of the "terrible Apache." Almost without exception these accounts are fakes, padded up to a semblance of truth by the introduction of incidents that actually occurred, but did not occur to the party glorified.

During the three years from May, 1882 to May, 1885, Al Sieber alone was Chief of Scouts. Until May, 1885, there were no civilian employees in any way connected with the management of the Indians except Sieber, MacIntosh, and Bowman. MacIntosh was dismissed in the fall of 1883. The reader can draw his own conclusions when he reads the historical romances of Tom, Bill, and Charley, if those romances refer to the periods I have mentioned. After the outbreak in May, 1885, other civilians were employed in various capacities connected with the pursuit of the hostiles. Of these I have no knowledge, as Sieber and I were in Mexico from May until September, when I went on leave of absence pending the acceptance of my resignation from the army.

Mickey Free, I do not class as a civilian. He was with me as interpreter continuously during all my term of service except for a short time in the winter of 1882-83, when he was in the field with Crawford, and on the General's expedition into Mexico.

The administrative personnel completed, our first

care was the organization of our scout companies and pack trains. In speaking of scouts I refer only to Indians. We used no civilians as scouts.

Five companies were enlisted under the designations of Companies A, B, C, D, and E. Each company ordinarily comprised a first sergeant, a second sergeant, two corporals, and twenty-six privates. But the number of privates was largely increased and additional sergeants and corporals appointed in such emergencies as the General's expedition to Mexico, when four companies numbered nearly two hundred men with an additional sergeant and two additional corporals to each company.

The sergeants and corporals were appointed by Crawford from the chiefs and prominent men. As far as possible Indians from the same tribe were enlisted in the same company. Company A, for duty with Gatewood at Fort Apache, was composed entirely of White Mountain. The other companies were to some extent mixed until the Chiricahua were all back on the Reservation. Company B was then entirely made up of Chiricahua and Warm Springs for duty under me at Turkey Creek.

In addition to the regular scout enlistments seven secret scouts were enlisted from the most trustworthy Indians we could find to take the dangerous job. Two of these were for Gatewood at Fort Apache. Of those at San Carlos, two were women. One woman and one man went with me later to Turkey Creek.

The duty of these scouts was to report to us every indication of discontent or hostility that might arise among the Indians on the Reservation. They took no part in campaigns, but were employed solely to keep us posted on symptoms of unrest or agitations that might lead to serious difficulties in or between the various tribes, or even to outbreaks; a duty they performed thoroughly and faithfully, enabling us to nip in the bud many situations that might have led to serious trouble.

Their method of communicating with us was, of course, secret. A tap on a window pane shortly after our lights were out would bring the occupant of the room to the door. Communication with them was usually through Sieber or MacIntosh; with them away, through Mickey Free. Some of them spoke a little Spanish and occasionally came to me direct with their reports. This direct reporting became the usual thing at Turkey Creek as the Chiricahua secret service man and woman I had there distrusted Mickey, fearing that he might betray them to some of their friends.

If any of the Indians suspected the activities of these secret scouts they gave no intimation of it. Nor was any secret service scout advised that there were others. If they suspected each other, they kept their suspicions to themselves.

Following the organization of the scout companies all the Indians at or near San Carlos were ordered to the military headquarters there, where they were counted. To the males capable of bearing arms, which included all boys from about the age of fourteen up, brass identification tags were issued, which they were ordered always to keep on their person. On these tags were letters and numbers indicating the band to which the Indian belonged and his number in the band.

By this means, when any Indians were reported off the Reservation a count could be ordered and the guilty determined. It was not necessary to tag the women as the men were held responsible for them, and they never left the Reservation without the men.

The principal bands at San Carlos were the San Carlos, Tonto, Tonto-Mohave, Apache-Yuma, Mohave, and Yuma. Of the two latter bands there were only a few. They were a distinct people from the Apache proper, spoke a different language, wore their hair in a different style, and were readily distinguished from the Apache. They were peaceful, engaged in agriculture when they had a chance, and in their native state had lived in comparatively permanent villages.

The Tonto-Mohave and Apache-Yuma were Mohave and Yuma bands whose ancestors had intermarried with neighboring Apache tribes. They spoke both languages but their characteristics were mainly Apache.

At Fort Apache the White Mountain, Coyotero, and Cibucu bands of Apache under Gatewood were similarly counted and the males tagged. The Coyotero were a small band, twelve or fifteen families, a connecting link between the White Mountain bands and the hostile Chiricahua. When I moved to Turkey Creek with the Chiricahua and Warm Springs in the summer of 1884 most of the Coyotero joined my camp.

The count at San Carlos, about 4,000, and Fort Apache about 1,500, gave a total of about 5,500 Indians on the Reservation, of whom about 1,400 were males considered old enough to bear arms. The count at this time did not, of course, include the 500 Chiricahua and Warm Springs in Mexico.

When Crawford reported for duty at San Carlos he had left his troop, G of the Third Cavalry, at Fort Thomas, under command of his second lieutenant, Parker W. West. At Crawford's request to the General, West and the troop, about forty men, were transferred to San Carlos where, under tents and brush shelters, they remained until the Third Cavalry was transferred to Texas in the winter of 1884-85.

When in the winter of 1883 I was ordered out on what became permanent duty in the field during the remaining two years of my service, Lieutenants Elliot, Dugan, and Strother were successively detailed for duty at San Carlos. In the early spring of 1885 Captain Pierce of the First Infantry relieved Crawford, who had asked to be returned to duty with his troop, then in Texas.

Our organizations of the scout companies completed and the Indians counted, the several pack trains in the Department were sent to San Carlos for reorganization and equipment. These were formed into five trains of forty packs, each under a chief packer, and ten packers for a crew. New equipment was purchased, worn out or unserviceable mules were replaced, and everything was put in the best possible shape for hard work when called for. The General's hobby, if he had one, was pack trains for Indian duty; and he insisted on the best in men, mules, and equipment that money and care, guided by experience, could provide.

Preliminaries out of the way, Crawford turned his attention to the complaints of the Indians. In addition to the Agency, under the direct control of the Agent, there was an Indian trader's store in a building two hundred yards to the north of the Agency building. The trader was under the control of the Agent if he saw fit to exercise control; which he did not. There the Indians were permitted to purchase certain articles, in trade or cash, when they had anything to exchange for the trader's goods. The trader fixed the prices on what he sold and the Indians could "take it or leave it." They were not allowed to leave the Reservation, and thus were at his mercy. After Crawford had a talk with him, prices were cut practically in half.

The Indians had complained to the General of the quality and quantity of beef issued to them. Crawford ordered me to investigate the deliveries and report to him. About a hundred yards east of the Agency was an adobe corral with a small slaughterhouse attached to it. This latter was used only to slaughter for the Americans at the Agency. The beeves for the Indian ration were held on herd a few miles from the Agency. Once a week the required number were cut out of the herd, driven to the Agency, weighed on a stock scale, and turned into the corral. An Indian policeman with a rifle stood on the adobe wall of the corral and shot the beeves down. When all for that day had been killed the women and children with two or three men fell upon them with knives, skinning them and cutting them up. The police saw to it that a more or less fair division was made of the meat among the families who sent for their share; the division, however, was not without the usual fighting and squabbling of the old women over choice bits of organs and entrails.

So far as Colonel Beaumont, the agency clerk, knew, the scales had never been tested. From the quartermaster's department at Fort Thomas I obtained a dozen fifty-pound test weights. A test of the scales revealed that the contractor was getting paid every week for about 1,500 pounds of beef that he did not deliver.

The beef herd was kept south of the Gila River. The slaughter pen was north of it. Deliveries were made about sunrise. To reach the pen, the beeves had to cross the river. Having had no water since some time the day before, they stopped and filled up just before being weighed. In that hot, dry climate they came on the scales looking like miniature Zeppelins. The Government was paying a pretty stiff price for half a barrel of Gila River water delivered with each beef.

There was not enough fat on the animals to fry a jackrabbit, many of them being mere skin and bones. I charged the herders with bringing some of them to the pen on their ponies, but they denied it, insisting that the animals had actually walked there. The contractor was dismissed and the contract let to Mr. H. C. Hooker, a prominent cattleman with a ranch just west of Camp Grant. We had no more complaints on the score of meat.

The General desired especially to get the Indians at occupations of some sort that would enable them to earn at least a portion of their keep; and, perhaps, in time lay the foundation for their self-support. A few of them had been making a feeble effort at raising a little grain in the river bottoms; but even this had been discouraged by the previous agents in the interest of civilians who were selling supplies to the Agency at fabulous prices. With no facilities in the way of proper implements; no irrigating ditches, in a country where irrigation was an absolute necessity; no knowledge of farming, except the little possessed by the few Yuma and Mohave, all efforts at accomplishing anything had been abandoned.

A feeling of restlessness, discontent, fear, and uncertainty for the future possessed the entire people. The attitude of all was that of watchful waiting, wondering what was going to turn up next. Once a week the women and children gathered at the Agency to receive the rations doled out to them. Returning to their wikiups, they waited stoically for the next ration day. Many families, with the improvidence the Indian had inherited from past generations, consumed in four or five days the rations for the week; for the remaining two or three days they begged from the more provident; lived on rabbits, rats, birds, and herbs, if fortunate in getting them, or went hungry. The men spent their time in idleness, trivial gambling at Indian games, or nightly dances when the larder was full. At San Carlos there was nothing to hunt except an occasional rabbit or rat, so that effort was left to the small boy with bow and arrow.

The White Mountain and Cibucu near Fort Apache were far more fortunate. They were nearly self-supporting, raised quite a little grain, and the mountains in which they lived were a game paradise abounding in deer, turkeys (which they did not eat), bear, and an occasional elk. Bear meat they ate only in times of stress, and fish not at all, although the streams near Fort Apache were swarming with mountain trout. These Indians were near of kin to the Navaho and much like them in their habits—herdsmen rather than agriculturists.

The stationing at San Carlos of the cavalry troop and three of the five pack trains (one had gone to the General at Whipple and one to Gatewood at Fort Apache), afforded an opportunity for immediate occupation to such Indians as desired it. As quartermaster I was instructed to purchase from the Indians hay for the horses and mules. The order was given lightly, but when I next saw the General and told him what he had let me in for, taciturn as he was, he laughed out loud. But it was no laughing matter for me.

I was to pay for the hay at a cent a pound. My only means of weighing it was on a platform scale that would weigh up to three hundred pounds. The Indians cut the hay, wild black gamma grass, with butcher knives and tied it into bundles weighing from fifteen to forty or fifty pounds. This work was done almost entirely by the women and children, only a few of the men deigning to take part in it.

The grass grew in small clumps around and in the scrubby mesquite and sage bushes of the upland mesas. As hay it is unexcelled. Some of the women and children trudged several miles with their bundles on their backs. Others, more fortunate, formed combinations and brought the larger portion of their burdens on a community pony; but each bundle had to be weighed and paid for separately, even if two or more bundles belonged to the same person. A detail from the scouts opened the bundles and put the hay in stack.

One fine-looking young woman would have been a wealthy contractor in a civilized country. She was a widow with two children, a boy and a girl, about eight or ten years of age. From other Indians she rented three ponies and every other day came in with 200 to 250 pounds of hay on two of the ponies; she, the children, and more bundles on the third.

The job of weighing and paying for four or five hundred small bundles of hay every afternoon was enough in itself; but the old women, and some of the younger ones, had to add to my misery. To beat me on weights they resorted to all the tricks in the calendar. Every bundle had to be searched for rocks, pieces of heavy mesquite, or bunches of water-soaked leaves or grass stuffed inside. When a culprit was detected, especially if an old woman, I was called all the names in the Spanish dictionary, and in addition such choice ones as had been learned from the American packers. The Apache had no oaths in their own language; they had to borrow from us or from the Mexicans.

The few Indian men accepted my weights without question; but the women, quickly learning the meaning of the scale, insisted on "down weights," and then some for good measure. Crawford told me to take the worst of it. I took it, and got it. Only silver dimes, quarters, and halves were used in payment. No nickels. Overpayment was, of course, the rule. Purchases went on all that fall and into the winter. By spring I had several hundred tons of hay in stack that mules and horses left their grain to eat. But when my stack was gone a board of survey had to relieve me of a shortage of nearly fifty tons.

With the advent of cold weather wood was added to my purchases. The men now began to wake up and we soon had several little contracts working. The wood was bought by the cord, a different price being paid for cottonwood and for mesquite.

With just rationing, fair prices in the trader's store, and a little money to buy the simple things they craved, the rancor of the Indians quickly faded away. Little children no longer fled from us. The women began to appear in fresh, clean clothes; laughing, joking, jollying, and scolding the scouts when detected with a surreptitious foot on the scales. Weighing hay became an afternoon diversion. The trader's store kept open till nine o'clock at night and was as crowded as a curio shop on a bargain day. A laughing, chattering, happy crowd. Children wakened from a nightmare!

The men sought us for talks and cigarettes. We were getting their confidence, of all things the most necessary to our control of them.

Shortly after we took over control of the Reservation

two young men who had just graduated from one of the Indian schools in the East reported to Crawford. He asked them what they proposed to do now that they were back among their people. One had learned the cobbler's trade, one that of a carpenter.

"Well," explained the spokesman of the two, "we have talk that over. They say at school, when you go back among Indians you tell Indians 'bout Jesus. So we think we tell Indians 'bout Jesus. That more better."

This was hardly the answer Crawford expected, but curious to see the outcome he gave them a room in a small building near the Agency and put them on the pay roll as scouts.

A few weeks later Sieber, up late at night, noticed a light shining through their window. Curious to know what kept them up after midnight, Sieber investigated. Through the window he was entertained with an Apache dance performed by the two young men and two young women, all hilariously drunk and garbed as nature garbed them. In the morning Crawford stopped their pay, sent them to their tribes, and left them to their own resources with a reminder that corn must be grown before it can be consumed in liquid form.

I do not wish these young men to be accepted as a type of graduate of our Indian schools, even at that early date. They were an exception, as were the circumstances under which they fell. Among the earliest of such graduates, the first, as I remember, among the Apache, they returned from school to find themselves ostracized by even their own families. Much might be said in excuse of their offense, and I mention the incident only to show the temptation and circumstances under which the Indian so frequently lapsed.

An incident shortly occurred that, beginning and ending in tragedy, tested the cardinal principle of the General's theory of Indian control. In his talk with the chiefs he had impressed upon them the fact that they must themselves control their people; that the scouts were for use against armed bands of hostiles and preserving the peace of the Reservation, and individual cases of crimes against Indians must be dealt with by the tribe to which the Indian belonged. He, the General, would look to the tribe for the arrest and punishment of the offender, using the scouts only when the tribe failed.

An Indian of a San Carlos band murdered his wife and took to the hills. Crawford sent for the head men of the band, reminded them of the General's orders, and demanded that they produce the murderer. Two or three days later he was brought to headquarters.

Crawford decided on a trial by jury of twelve men from his own tribe. The trial took place in the schoolhouse in the presence of about a hundred of the San Carlos Apache, Indians of the other tribes remaining away. The accused defiantly admitted his guilt, and refused to explain the reason for his act or to offer anything in palliation. The jury found him guilty and condemned him to death, explaining that under Indian custom the relatives of the woman would have killed him when opportunity offered. Such opportunities were just what the General wished to avoid, as they led often to reprisal, and eventually to war, between tribes.

The verdict rendered, Crawford came over to our office, where I was engaged in some routine work, and told me the result, adding: "Davis, I can't turn this man over to the Indians to execute. It will only cause more trouble. We have got to attend to it ourselves. I so hate the thought of it that I wish you would have it done and not let me know anything about it." Then he went to his room and closed the door.

Crawford was a man of the highest courage, and like all men of high courage he had the heart of a motherly woman. I could well understand his feelings. Having presided at the trial, talked to the prisoner before trial, and vainly tried to find in his own mind some excuse that would mitigate the offense, sentiment had gripped him. I had not been harried by this experience and felt no personal sentiment.

We had at headquarters a light, four-mule wagon with a high spring-seat for the driver. The driver was an old prospector working during the winter months for a "grub stake." A little after dark he was ordered to hitch up his team. The prisoner was told that he was to be sent to Fort Thomas. He was put in the body of the wagon with two armed guards, not of his band, from one of the scout companies. He had been shackled as soon as he was condemned. Sieber took a seat beside the driver.

A few miles from San Carlos, as they were crossing a sandbar, the prisoner asleep in his blankets on the floor of the wagon, Sieber reached down with his revolver and shot him through the head. His body was buried in the sand and the execution party returned to San Carlos. I made no report to Crawford, not so much as a hint that the sentence had been executed, and he never referred to it.

The rôle of executioner was not a nerve-racking one to Sieber. He had had previous experience. Of one instance he told me himself in a humorous vein, so I accept it as authentic.

Some years before I knew him he was out with a troop

of cavalry hunting hostile Apache. The command had a brush with a small band of them, the principal result of which was the capture of one lone Indian. The command had been out quite a while on the scout, were at a considerable distance from any source of supplies, and rations were very low. As they were breaking camp the morning after the capture, Sieber heard the officer in command express regret that they had a captive who had to be fed and guarded until they reached a military post.

"Don't mind him, I'll take care of him," offered Sieber; and the command moved out leaving Sieber, the captive, and a trooper who had been on night guard to follow.

The trooper was crouched by the embers of the cook's fire, eating his breakfast; the Indian, his breakfast finished, was crouched beside him smoking a cigarette. Sieber walked up behind the Indian and shot him through the head. As the body pitched forward into the fire the trooper merely glanced up at Sieber with the protest:

"Say, Al, if you were going to do that why in hell didn't you do it before he got his belly full of grub!" and went on with his breakfast.

Such was the callousness with which the white man had come to regard the taking of the red man's life. Exasperated, our senses blunted by Indian atrocities, we hunted them and killed them as we hunted and killed wolves.

The General directed that several of the principal Indians be selected and sent East, to bring back tales of the white man's power and the futility of the Indian's efforts to oppose it. Years before, the eldest son of the great Apache captain, Cochise, had gone to Washington with a delegation of Apache and had died there. His body rests in Arlington Cemetery. With this in mind, none of the Indians now evinced any enthusiasm when again offered a sight-seeing tour at Uncle Sam's expense. The sentiment was universal to "let George do it." Finally, however, a party of eight or ten was made up and sent on their way in charge of Lieutenant West. They were taken to Washington and to New York City on a tour that lasted several weeks.

On their return, I questioned some of them and formed the opinion that West was the only one of the party who had enjoyed himself. One of the chiefs told me that on leaving he had determined to count all the white people he saw on the trip. At Willcox, the railroad station, he decided to count only the wikiups (houses). Later, on the train, he confined the count to rancherias (towns), but soon ran out of Indian numerals and gave up counting.

In New York City they were quartered in an upper room of the Fifth Avenue Hotel. Some of them, leaning out of a window and gazing at the people on the street below, asked West why these people were walking round and round the hotel? When West explained that they were not the same people, but different ones passing by, they told him he was lying to have some fun with them.

So far as impressing the Indians of the Reservation was concerned, the trip was a failure. The delegates were denounced as liars who had been corrupted by the white man, and for a time were avoided as though they had the plague. One of them went insane and several were long in recovering from a sort of daze, refusing to discuss what they had seen. They had, of course, no words to describe much of it, even had they desired to do so.

On the southern edge of the Reservation a vein of impure coal had been discovered. The agency trader and others had attempted to establish claims on it with a view to selling their claims to the Southern Pacific Railroad, which had shortly before completed its east-west line. The coal was worthless, but the attempts were causing us trouble.

The Indians reported that two Americans had established a camp on the coal vein about two miles within the reservation borders. Al Sieber and two or three scouts were sent to bring the men to San Carlos. Crawford told them that it was against the law establishing the Reservation for unauthorized persons to remain on it and that he would have to put them off. The men laughed.

"Captain," said one of them, "we are only two miles from the line, it won't be far to walk."

Crawford turned to me with a gleam of keen amusement in his eyes.

"Davis," he ordered, "have that light wagon hitched up. I think those mules need exercise."

The men and their belongings were loaded into the wagon and put off the Reservation north of Fort Apache, on the road to Holbrook. The only transportation between the Reservation and the railroad was by military conveyances. The men had in view a forty-five-mile hike to the railroad at Holbrook, a 500-mile rail journey, and another hike of a hundred miles to get back to their camp at the coal vein. They did not come back.

To me, the most striking characteristic of the Apache was his utter disregard of consequences when excited or enraged. This trait of character was doubtless what made him such a desperate fighter when cornered. When at war with his enemies, the Apache took no unnecessary chances. His long suits were ambuscade, sudden attacks on the defenseless, and flight from superior numbers. Corner him, and he was madness personified.

These berserker rages would break out at times in individuals without, so far as we could ever learn, any reason for them. Inexplicable crimes would be committed under their influence. The Indians themselves seemed to take them as a matter of course and to our questioning as to why so-and-so had committed the crime, or taken to the hills to be hunted down like a mad dog, the only answer we were likely to get would be a shrug of the shoulders and, "Don't know. Just mad." Before a civil jury the verdict would be temporary insanity. But in the Apache it was not insanity; it was just uncontrolled temper throwing consequences into the discard.

Sieber and I were sitting by the agency building talking to Colonel Beaumont late one afternoon. A little to our left the mesa on which the buildings stood fell off to the river bottom below in a ridge that extended to the agency guardhouse, some two hundred yards in front of us. It was customary to bring the prisoners out late every afternoon to meet their relatives and receive any little delicacies or clean clothing brought to them. The meeting place was along the edge of the ridge. An armed guard accompanied them and the more dangerous of them were shackled about the feet.

Suddenly we saw a commotion on the ridge. Something was going on just below it, out of our sight. We saw the guard raise his rifle as though to fire. As we ran toward him Sieber began shouting to him in Indian: "Fire! Fire!"

Again he raised his gun and lowered it; then raised it and fired.

When we reached him we saw just below the ridge the body of a young Indian lying partly across the body of a young woman, the man with shackles on his ankles and a bullet hole just below his right armpit. The woman had the hilt of a knife sticking out of her left side. Both were dead. From the guard we learned what had happened.

They were man and wife. She had brought him a change of clothing and was in the act of handing it to him when he snatched a knife she had on a belt around her waist and began stabbing her in the side over the heart, keeping her between him and the guard. The point of the knife, an ordinary butcher knife, was dull, and striking the ribs, would not penetrate. The guard, meanwhile, was trying to shoot, but was not able to do so without hitting the woman. Finally the knife entered and the man churned it around in her body, killing her instantly. As she fell the man exposed his side and the guard shot him through the heart, killing him instantly also.

What was the reason for the double tragedy? We never could find out. The same indifferent answer to our inquiries, "Don't know. Maybe mad." There were no attempts at reprisal on the part of the relatives of either, and so far as we could learn from the secret service scouts not even any ill feeling or excitement among them. "Why talk about them? They are both dead. How many beeves will be issued next ration day?"

Chapter IV

Crawford leaves for a scout along the Mexican border. The General prepares to rout the hostiles out of their stronghold in the Mexican mountains. Hostiles under Chato and Benito raid north from Mexico. Judge McComas and his wife killed. The capture of Tzoe. He guides the expedition into Mexico. I am left in military control of the Reservation. Arrest of a man charged with selling liquor to Indians. Es-ki-mo-tzin and his fate. An Indian feast. Pat Keogh.

IN the latter part of October, our organization being completed, the General ordered Crawford to take the field with three of the companies of Indian scouts—C, D, and E,—leaving me in charge of matters with Company B at San Carlos and Gatewood with Company A at Fort Apache. We had heard nothing from the hostiles in Mexico except an occasional rumor that one or two had been seen near the Reservation seeking information or cartridges. Crawford was directed to take station near Cloverdale, Arizona, and by sending a few scouts down into Mexico find out where the hostiles were and what they were doing. Three of the scouts went as far as sixty miles south of the international border but could get no information worth while.

In March, 1883, the General began organizing for an expedition into Mexico to rout the hostiles out. Permission to cross the border had been granted by the Mexican Government. While the expedition was being organized the Tombstone Rangers, of the same general character as the Globe Rangers and under the same or a better brand of stimulant, set out to massacre all the Indians on the Reservation. At the camp of Es-ki-mo-tzin on the southern edge of the Reservation, they met with an old Indian who was gathering mescal for a mescal bake. They fired at him, but fortunately missed. He fled north and they fled south. That ended the massacre.

We were constantly expecting a raid from the hostiles in Mexico. Near the end of March, as the General's expedition was assembling, our expectations were realized. Crawford, Gatewood, Sieber, MacIntosh, and Mickey Free were at Willcox, Arizona, where the General with Crawford's and Gatewood's scouts and a detachment of cavalry was preparing to enter Mexico. On March 24 I received a telegram from the General saying that a body of hostiles, fifteen or twenty in number, had crossed the international border and were headed north. I was directed to be on the lookout for them should they enter the Reservation, and to warn the friendly Indians not to harbor them. Bowman had been left with me at San Carlos as chief of scouts and interpreter.

When the Indians were notified that a war party of Chiricahua were on their way toward the Agency, the clusters of women and children that were accustomed to congregate daily around the agency buildings, our quarters, and the trader's store, disappeared. The Indian villages took on the appearance of armed camps. Guns and ammunition we had never suspected the Indians of having were produced, and a number of armed Tonto and San Carlos Apache voluntarily took up the task of outposts in the neighboring hills.

The night of March 28 I was advised by telegram that the hostiles had killed Judge McComas and his wife near Silver City, New Mexico, and had carried off their six-year-old son, Charley. They were reported to have then headed west and might be expected to attack at some point of the Reservation within the next day, or day following at most, as they were traveling rapidly. It was supposed that their objects were primarily to induce other disaffected bands to join them; and secondarily, to obtain ammunition, of which they were greatly in need on account of their constant warfare with the Mexicans.

Suspense is hard to bear in the face of threatened attack, as I found out during the following sixty hours, and I slept with one eye and half the other open. I knew what had happened the previous spring, when a party of Chiricahua came up from Mexico and took out Loco and his people. There were still many hundred disaffected Indians on the Reservation. If another outbreak should occur the massacre of all the whites at the Agency was not at all improbable.

The door to my room was at the foot of my bed. Beyond the bed and at right angles to it was a large window, against which anyone entering the room at night was in plain view from the bed. About midnight of the thirtieth I had just turned in, when I heard the hinges of the door creak and on looking up saw the form of an Indian as he noiselessly entered the room, gun in hand. My revolver was on the bed beside me and I covered him with it as I asked who he was.

"Tar-gar-de-chuse," he replied, in an excited whisper —one of our secret service men—"Chiricahua come," he continued.

I bounced out of bed and got Bowman. Tar-gar-de-chuse reported that the Chiricahua were in the camp of three or four White Mountain Apache up the San Carlos River, about twelve or fourteen miles from the

Agency. He did not know how many they were. I had thirty scouts, scattered in the camps near the Agency. When they were assembled half an hour later they were joined by five or six armed Tonto volunteers who had some especial grudge against the hostiles. If these latter were "fifteen or twenty," as reported, we could count on outnumbering them two to one.

There was no moon, but the night was bright starlight. We were all afoot and after half the distance from the Agency had been covered, we moved cautiously. Indian "underground telegrams," by which the information had come, are not always reliable, and the hostiles might be in some other camp. Half a mile from the camp of the White Mountain we halted to wait for daylight, just beginning to break. Then we moved up to the edge of the little clearing in which the camp was located and formed a half circle around it, with the protection of such scrubby trees and mounds as the ground afforded.

My first sergeant called to the people in the camp, none of whom were in sight. From one of the wikiups a man's voice answered. I do not know what was said, but my scouts at once moved forward, surrounded the camp, and captured—one lone Chiricahua. And he was not a Chiricahua, but a White Mountain married to a Chiricahua. He was, however, one of the hostiles; a handsome young fellow about twenty-three or twenty-four years of age, known to the Indians as Tzoe, but called Peaches by the whites on account of his peach-like complexion.

He said he had left the hostiles near the eastern edge of the Reservation and had come to this White Mountain camp to get news of his mother and other members of his family. He seemed little disturbed by his capture and smiled faintly when I took his knife and cartridge belt off of him. My scouts had his rifle.

I learned from him that the hostiles numbered twenty-six in all under the subchiefs Chato and Benito. A year or so later, after their surrender, I learned from some of these raiders themselves that on this raid, where they traveled horseback some 400 to 450 miles during the six days and nights they were in the United States, Chato got no sleep except what he could take on his horse while riding. When the party stopped to rest he stood guard. They changed their mounts frequently for horses they stole from the ranches *en route*.

This party was armed, as in fact were nearly all the hostiles in Mexico, with the latest models of Winchester magazine rifles, a better arm than the single shot Springfield with which our soldiers and scouts were armed. The Indians obtained their arms from settlers and travelers they killed, or purchased them from white scoundrels who made a business of selling arms, ammunition, and whiskey to Indians.

I took Tzoe to our headquarters at the Agency and wired the General at Willcox of the capture. He instructed me to find out if Tzoe would consent to act as a guide for his expedition, then about to start for Mexico. Tzoe consented readily and I sent him to Willcox. He proved faithful, efficient, and of great service in saving the command unnecessary hardship, and contributed largely to the success of the expedition.

With the departure for Mexico of the General, Crawford, Gatewood, Sieber, MacIntosh, and Mickey Free, the responsibility of maintaining order during the ensuing two months among five thousand restless, idle, turbulent Apache fell upon the shoulders of a "shave-tail" second lieutenant not quite out of his army swaddling clothes. My only assistant was Sam Bowman, who had been left with me as interpreter. Crawford's troop of cavalry, about forty men under West, had, however, been left at the Agency.

Fortunately only one incident occurred that gave me any concern. A report came to me that a white man who had a small cabin near the southern border of the Reservation was selling whiskey and ammunition to the Indians. With the report came another, that he had said he would "shoot hell out of any damned army officer who attempted to arrest him."

I walked into his cabin one morning about sunrise with two of my scouts. He was stooping by the hearth of his fireplace cooking his breakfast, with his rifle within easy reach, but he made no effort to use it. On the contrary, he glanced up with a smile and asked me if I had had breakfast.

"Bin expectin' you," he said.

I turned the rifle over to one of my scouts and had breakfast with him. We were soon on the best of terms. I told him I had to take him to Tucson for trial, and he laughed at it as a good joke on me. Said they would do nothing with him when I got him there. He was right. The U.S. Marshal and the District Attorney were very enthusiastic over the arrest. They congratulated me and assured me the man would be made an example of. Such offenses "imperiled the lives of citizens, etc., etc."

As I bade my prisoner goodbye on his way to jail he said he would be around to have a drink with me at the hotel in half an hour. He kept the appointment and that was the last I ever heard of the case.

On my way to Tucson with this man I passed through

the camp of an Indian known as Es-ki-mo-tzin, who is worthy of more than passing notice. If the day ever comes when the white man can find it in his heart to really sympathize with the red man, a volume can be written of Es-ki-mo-tzin and his little band of followers that will excel in pathos and tragedy anything ever conceived by Fenimore Cooper. I can only briefly refer to it here.

In the early seventies Es-ki-mo-tzin was a determined enemy of the whites and Mexicans. With a small band of followers he remained in the mountains, refusing all overtures at making peace with him. One by one a follower here and there, tired of continual warfare, deserted him and sued for peace; but Es-ki-mo-tzin stubbornly held out, escaping all efforts made to entrap him.

Some few miles from Old Camp Grant there lived a trapper, the only white man Es-ki-mo-tzin called a friend and the only one he trusted. At this man's cabin he would occasionally stop for food and shelter. One night he stopped there, had breakfast with his friend in the morning, then, as he was leaving, turned and shot him down.

Finally he was captured. Asked why he had killed his only white friend, he replied:

"To teach my people that there must be no friendship between them and the white men. Anyone can kill an enemy, but it takes a strong man to kill a friend." Various writers have quoted Es-ki-mo-tzin's statement in various ways. The statement above is virtually as given me by Sam Bowman, who knew him well.

New Camp Grant was being built. Es-ki-mo-tzin and a few members of his band who had been captured with him were put to work, in irons, making adobes for the new post. After three years of hard labor he begged for liberty and a return to the Reservation, but asked that a little plot of ground be assigned to him and his immediate followers apart from the mass of Indians at San Carlos, who were still idle and uneasy.

Desert lands in Arizona in the early seventies were considered worth about a thousand dollars less than nothing. The Reservation lines had never been accurately surveyed. Es-ki-mo-tzin and his band, by order of General O. O. Howard, representing the Indian Bureau, were given a small section of bottom land near the mouth of a small stream, the San Pedro, that emptied into the Gila just below the Agency. This land was supposed to be within the lines of the Reservation. When I visited their camp on my way to Tucson with my prisoner the Indians had occupied the ground about ten years.

As I was passing the camp Es-ki-mo-tzin came out and stopped me, insisting that I remain for dinner with him, letting my Indians with Bowman and the prisoner go on. After dinner we would overtake them in his buggy. Curious to see what progress the Indians had made on the road to civilization, I consented. What I saw I would not have believed Indians capable of under at least one more generation.

The little colony of six or eight families might well be mistaken for a colony of prosperous Mexican farmers. They had adobe houses, fields under barbed wire fences, modern (for those days) farming implements, good teams, and cows. They dressed as the Mexicans in Arizona dressed—cotton shirt and trousers for field work, a suit of "store clothes" for important affairs; dances, Sundays, feast days, etc.

In Es-ki-mo-tzin's house a greater surprise was in store for me. His wife and children in their Sunday best of bright calicos were introduced to me. The dinner table was set in the living-room with a clean white cover; plates, cups, knives, forks, and spoons at each place. Substantial chairs for the grown-ups, four of us. Mrs. Es-ki-mo-tzin and the younger children served the meal, a very well-cooked and appetizing one as I remember it. For the occasion Es-ki-mo-tzin had on his store suit of coat, vest, and trousers; adding to it a near-gold watch with a heavy silver chain, of which he was very proud, and by which he had learned to tell the time after a fashion.

Dinner over, a young man appeared with a light buggy and a remarkably good team of small horses, well kept and eager to go. Es-ki-mo-tzin proved himself a skilful driver and we overtook Bowman and the scouts before they made camp. The following morning, as we were preparing to take the road to Tucson, Es-ki-mo-tzin again drove up and insisted on taking me into Tucson, leaving the others to follow.

At Tucson he took me to see several merchants with whom he did business. These men told me that Es-ki-mo-tzin frequently ran accounts in Tucson totaling several thousand dollars, and that his credit was good for four or five thousand in the principal store there should he desire it for himself or his people.

At this time the agitation over the coal supposed to be on the southern edge of the Reservation was in full cry. To it was added an effort to get the land occupied by Es-ki-mo-tzin and his people. It was claimed that their farms were south of the reservation line. The lines of the Reservation had never been accurately surveyed, but

Es-ki-mo-tzin and his people had been located where they were by duly constituted officials of our government, with full power to assign to them any plot of ground they might select in the then Territory of Arizona.

So long as General Crook remained in Arizona his influence prevented the infamy; but not long after he was relieved by General Miles, Es-ki-mo-tzin and his people were removed to San Carlos, and their homes, farms, and all fixed improvements turned over to white settlers. Es-ki-mo-tzin died shortly thereafter.

One incident throws a light on the character of this remarkable man. When he came over to meet the General at San Carlos in September, 1882, the General asked him how he was getting along with the white people with whom he came in contact. He had learned a little English, of which he was very proud. With some aid from the interpreter, this was his reply:

"When first go San Pedro white man pass by, look back over shoulder, say 'There go ol' Skimmy.' Now white man pass by, raise hat, say 'Good morning Mr. Skimmotzin.'"

On our way back from Tucson to the Agency we camped for the night near a large pile of brush. My Indians immediately laid aside their rifles and cartridge belts, cut long, limber sticks, surrounded the brush pile, and set fire to it. In a few minutes rats began to run from the burning brush in every direction; the Indians, yelling and laughing like a lot of school boys at a football game, killed the rats as they ran out. By the time the brush was consumed the Indians had a matter of two dozen rats. A camp kettle of boiling water was on another fire. Into it went the rats without previous preparation. When they were considered done to Indian taste a sharp stick was thrust into the pot, a rat impaled and lifted out. Hide and hair came off in one operation; a slash of a knife for disemboweling, and the feast was ready.

I had been sitting on my bed roll near the fire watching the fun. The sergeant of my company came to me with the nicely skinned hind legs of an especially fat and juicy rat. At least the sergeant said it was especially fat and juicy. The rest of the scouts were grinning broadly as they watched to see what I would do, a newcomer among them. There was but one thing to do, and I did it —called the sergeant's bluff and ate rat. To my surprise I found the morsel quite good, much like very tender chicken or frog legs. But I did not ask for a second helping.

While there are several species of rodents in the Southwest this species of rat is the only rodent I ever saw the Indians enthuse over. Ground squirrels and gophers they ignored, except in periods of stress; but the discovery of one of these rat nests near a camping place was a signal for a feast.

Pat Keogh's pack train was left with me when Crawford took the field. Pat was as native to the "ould sod" as his name implies, and a book might be written about him. The following story is typical:

Pat with his train and a cargo of supplies was ordered to accompany Lieutenant Dorr from Fort Thomas to Fort Apache. *En route* it was necessary to cross Black River, a mountain torrent that at times was impassable, but which could be crossed at a moderate stage of high water by keeping the mules on a submerged ledge of rock that cut the stream like a dam. If, however, a mule got a little too far down stream he would go off the ledge into ten feet of water running like a mill race. We had a tradition in the army that a mule would take pretty good care of himself in water as long as he kept his head above it and did not get it into his ears. But let that disaster happen to him and subsequent proceedings interested him no more. He would at once give up the struggle, turn over on his side, and float calmly off to whatever mule heaven was awaiting him.

Pat and Dorr arrived at the river during one of these moderately high-water stages and started crossing the mules on the rock ledge. The packers of Pat's train were nearly all Mexicans, as were in fact the crews of all our trains. Pat and Dorr were standing on the bank of the stream watching the mules cross. A mule got too far downstream, went off the rock ledge, and in a moment was struggling in the torrent of deep water. Dorr yelled to Pat, who was nearest the mule:

"Pat! Pat! Jump in and hold his head up!"

"Jump in be domned," said Pat, with a look of disgust at Dorr, as he turned and walked away from the raging stream; "sind a Mixican. Arizony's full of Mixicans but there's only one Pat Keogh."

Chapter V

The General's expedition. Fate of Charley McComas. The hostiles agree to return to the Reservation. Arrival at San Carlos of some of them. Release of captive Mexican women. Ka-ya-ten-nae. Juh's daughter. Apache warfare. Celerity of movement. Ineffectual Mexican troops. I am ordered to the border. "Something to catch." Arrival at border of Zele and Nachite followed later by Chato and Mangus.

THE General's expedition into Mexico has been described in detail by Captain John G. Bourke, of the Third Cavalry, then on the General's staff, in his book *An Apache Campaign*. I need only describe it briefly for a better understanding of its bearing on my own experiences later.

The following is a complete list of the officers of the expedition and of such civilians as had any prominent part in it: General Crook; Captains Crawford, Bourke, and Chaffee; Lieutenants Gatewood, West, Forsyth, Febiger, and Mackay; Doctor Andrews.

The civilians were Sieber as Chief of Scouts, MacIntosh as assistant; Mickey Free and Severiano as interpreters.

With about two hundred Apache scouts enlisted from among the friendly Indians of the Reservation, a troop of cavalry, and two pack trains the General entered Mexico early in April. Under the guidance of Tzoe the expedition penetrated the Sierra Madre Mountains without their presence becoming known to the hostiles. About sixty miles northeast of the town of Nacori in

Sonora the main body of the expedition was halted and Crawford, with Gatewood and forty or fifty of the scouts, sent forward with Tzoe to reconnoiter. They surprised the camp of Benito while most of the men were away with a war party raiding Mexican settlements, killed several of the occupants of the camp, and captured several women and children.

Little Charley McComas was in the camp when it was attacked, but he either ran away in fright and subsequently perished in the mountains, or was killed at some distance from the camp by the fleeing women. The former I think more probable, as the Indians made no attempt to kill another small boy captive, who was with them when they reached San Carlos. This child, about six years of age, Crawford at first thought might be Charley; but Charley's uncle, who came to the Agency to identify him, decided that he was not Charley. He was subsequently identified as a Mexican child from the northern part of New Mexico and was restored to an uncle who came for him.

The war party returning from their raid on Mexican towns in Chihuahua were bringing with them five Mexican women captives. Seeing signs of the expedition they abandoned the women, who made their way into the General's camp. The poor things were in a state of collapse, and almost insane at their unexpected deliverance. Subsequently eight other Mexican women and children were turned over to the troops and later restored to their families in Mexico.

Through the Indian women that Crawford had captured, communication was established with the other camps of the hostiles and the chiefs were induced to come to the General's camp for a talk. The hostile camps were scattered over a tract of mountainous country some fifty miles square, much of it almost impregnable for troops. Two years later I spent three months scouting in it and found it hopeless for any sort of campaigning other than with Indians afoot.

The hostiles assured the General that they were tired of constant warfare. The fact that American troops with Indians of their own race had routed them out of their fastnesses in these Mexican mountains was a stunning blow to them. They wanted peace—in capital letters, so their sentiments might not be mistaken. They wanted to return to the Reservation at once and be "good Indian" for ever thereafter. "But," said the chiefs, "many of our people are scattered through the mountains in a dozen camps. It will take time to get word to them that peace has been declared. It will be especially difficult to get this word to them now as the alarm of the attack on Benito's camp has spread throughout the mountains."

It was finally agreed that the General should return to the United States with as many of the old men, women, and children as could be gotten together at once; some of the men to accompany them. The others to come in as soon as they could get word to the various rancherias and gather up their live stock. This they estimated would take about "two moons."

On June 23 the General arrived at San Carlos with 325 of the Chiricahua and Warm Spring bands; 52 men and 273 women and children. About two hundred, including most of the fighting men, had remained in Mexico, ostensibly to gather up the remnants of their people but in reality to raid Mexican ranches for horses to trade to the Indians of the Reservation.

Among the men who came in with the General were

the chiefs Nana and Loco, the subchief Benito, and a young man named Ka-ya-ten-nae, who, while not an hereditary chief, had gained great distinction as a warrior and was looked upon by the Indians as their coming war chief. He had never before been on a Reservation, was suspicious, disliked us thoroughly, and had counseled the Indians to fight it out in Mexico to the last rather than return to the United States. He had a personal following of thirty-two of the young men and became a trouble maker from the time he arrived. A year later, at Turkey Creek, he put me in the most critical situation I had to face in my three years among these people.

Among the women was a girl about eighteen years of age, the daughter of their former chief, Juh. A little more than a year before, when the Chiricahua had forced Loco and his people to leave the subagency, she was with the latter and in the fight with the Mexicans below the international border had been shot through the thigh. The wound had never healed; it had remained a running sore, and the limb below it had shriveled to mere bone and skin, as immovable as a rod of iron. Yet she had ridden and walked hundreds of miles with her people in their many changes of camps in Mexico, and rode the three hundred miles from near Nacori, Sonora, to San Carlos with them on this trip out with the General. She was hardly more than skin and bones herself but we had a hard time persuading her to let our surgeons amputate the limb; an amputation that restored her to health.

Her father, Juh, had been the successor of Cochise as head chief of the Chiricahua. The summer following Loco's departure from the subagency, Juh went in to the town of Casas Grandes in the northwestern part of Chihuahua, got drunk, and started back to his camp in the mountains. While attempting to swim a small stream in flood he fell from his mule and was drowned. Geronimo, although neither a chief nor a subchief, claimed his place but was accepted only by a small contingent of his own and Juh's personal following. I will have more to say of Geronimo later.

With the departure of the General and his staff for Whipple the scouts that had accompanied him to Mexico were discharged, with the exception of Company E. Company B that had remained with me at San Carlos, and Company A for duty with Gatewood at Fort Apache, constituted our force for maintaining order on the Reservation.

The advent of the Warm Springs and Chiricahua brought about a curious change in our relations with the Indians. Those who had come in were mostly Warm Springs. The greater portion of the Chiricahua still remained in Mexico under their hereditary chiefs, Mangus and Nachite, the subchiefs Chato and Zele, and the trouble maker, Geronimo.

Mangus, son of old Mangus Colorado, was hereditary chief of the Warm Springs, but on account of his pacific character he had been supplanted in the leadership of the tribe by Loco, a one-eyed Indian, after the death of Victorio, who had succeeded Mangus Colorado. Victorio's principal lieutenant had been Nana, now very old and partially crippled; but not old or crippled sufficiently to prevent his riding horseback ninety miles without rest, as I found out to my sorrow two years later.

In like manner Nachite, younger son of Cochise, had been supplanted, but for other reasons, first by Juh and on the latter's death by Geronimo. Nachite was a good warrior with no peace scruples; but he was fond of the ladies, liked dancing and a good time generally, and was not serious enough for the responsibilities of leadership. His brother, who had died in Washington, was said to have been an Indian of the finest type.

The Chiricahua and Warm Springs who had come in were temporarily located in the bottom lands of the San Carlos near our headquarters. Feared and hated by the other Indians of the Reservation, they seemed to turn to us for reassurance and comforting. Daily, half-a-dozen or more would be found hanging around our buildings, anxious for a talk and a smoke. Our relations with the other Indians had been rather formal. They came to us only when they had business with us and showed, with the exception of one or two of the scouts, no disposition to be chummy. The hostiles were different, and we soon came to feel toward some of them as we would feel toward any other class of people. In fact we began to find them decidedly human. Much to my surprise I found that they had a keen sense of humor and were not averse to telling jokes on themselves as well as on others. The tales of their adventures in their years of warfare against whites and Mexicans would fill volumes. One or two I will have occasion to relate later.

Two women whose families had been wiped out by incessant war practically adopted us to replace their lost relatives. They begged all our spare change to buy dresses and demanded that they be kept supplied with smoking materials. A little girl about seven or eight years of age became an especial *protégée* of West's. At his expense her mother decked her out in finery that would have done honor to any young Mexican señorita. These romantic friendships should have had the proper romantic ending—when the grateful Indian girl throws herself before the leveled rifles, *à la* Captain John Smith. But alas and alack! When the hostiles went out in the spring of 1885 the girl and the women went with them, seemingly not caring a trooper's damn whether I was filled full of lead or not.

Notable among the Indians who haunted our quarters was Ka-ya-ten-nae. But he made no effort to get on friendly terms with us. We would find him standing silent and alone near an open window, or at a corner of the building, or near a doorway; watchful, but surly and unresponsive when spoken to. Either he was exceptionally curious or exceptionally suspicious. Probably both. Reports were reaching us through the secret service that he regretted coming in and was disposed to make another break as soon as he could get a sufficiently strong following to make the attempt successful. I must in justice say of him, however, that after his incarceration in Alcatraz he became a very pleasant and companionable fellow and of great help to the General in his later dealings with the outlaws under Geronimo. This report of him I had from officers who met him after his release from prison. I did not again see him myself after I arrested him.

The newspapers of Arizona were full of abuse of the General for bringing these Indians back from Mexico. They were inciting the people of the territories to attack any other bands the General attempted to bring up, ignoring the fact that if they were not brought back where they could be kept under observation and control they would be constantly raiding up from Mexico, committing depredations, and returning to their stronghold in the almost impassable mountain ranges of the Sierra Madre.

The difficulties of subduing the Apache were so unique that they were not understood even by many of our superior officers in Washington. No one who had not been through the mill could understand them. General Sheridan, at that time in command of the army, was hopelessly at sea in his knowledge of these people, their mode of warfare, or the problem of catching them. His ignorance of these matters led him to give orders that were impossible to carry out. The impossibility of complying with one in particular, which I will quote later, resulted in Crook's replacement by Miles—and Miles could not comply with it.

The Apache was unlike any other Indian tribe the whites have ever fought since civilization began to creep over the North American continent. His mode of warfare was peculiarly his own. He saw no reason for fighting unless there was something tangible and immediate to be gained. To satisfy his pressing needs for arms, ammunition, food, or clothing he would raid isolated ranches, the suburbs of small Mexican towns, or ambush travelers. But he had no such sense of bravado as animated other Indian tribes who, resisting encroachment by the whites on the Indian's domain, fought us man to man in the open. His creed was "fight and run away, live to fight another day." Corner him, however, and you would find him as desperate and dangerous as a wounded wolf.

Only when cornered, or to delay pursuit of his women and children, would he engage a force anywhere near the strength of his own. To fight soldiers merely in defense of his country, he considered the height of folly; and he never committed that folly if he could avoid it. It is true that at Chevelon's Fork he stopped to fight Chaffee. But it was not a fight that he contemplated; it was to be an easy massacre of Chaffee's command.

With the General, only two-thirds of the hostiles had come in. There were still two hundred in Mexico who had promised to come as soon as they could do so. If the newspapers succeeded in inciting the people of the towns along the border to attack one of these bands on its way up from Mexico a disaster would be the result. Most of the Indians who had come in with the General would at once break away in an attempt to rejoin their friends and relatives below the border. With all precautions it would not be possible for us to prevent their doing so. We had before us the memory of the outbreaks of these same people in September, 1881 and May, 1882.

They were now better supplied with ponies than they had been on those two occasions; yet in 1881 and 1882 they had moved with such celerity, starting at a little before dark each time with their direction unknown, that it was impossible for the troops to entrap them. Such commands as did encounter them were stood off by the fighting men while the women and children continued on the race to the border. The fighting men would halt in a defensible position where the troops would have to dismount to attack them, fight the troops as long as they dared, then remount their ponies and at a run rejoin the women and children, by now ten or twelve miles ahead. As it was a stern chase for the troops, this process could be repeated as fast as troops overtook them. In forty-eight hours or less the Indians would be in Mexico, where the troops were not allowed to follow them. The General's expedition had been under an especial permit from the Mexican Government for this occasion only.

With the hostiles back in Mexico there could be no

peace on the border. Such raids as that of Chato would be frequently repeated; raiding some ranch of a late afternoon, and another the following morning; east, west, or north, a hundred miles away. The Mexicans were unwilling to make the sacrifices necessary to drive the Apache out of their stronghold in the Sierra Madre Mountains, on the border of the states of Chihuahua and Sonora. With a knowledge of the difficulties of such an undertaking, one could hardly blame them.

The Sierra Madre range south of the international border rose rapidly to an altitude of ten thousand to twelve thousand feet. On its western—Sonora—slope it fell off abruptly to an altitude of two thousand feet in about thirty miles as the crow flies. This slope was cut by deep and almost impassable cañons, with long ridges between them leading back to the crest of the range. After a raid on a Mexican town the Indians would retire up one of these ridges, from which they could see any pursuing force, and ambush and defeat or retard it. Driven from one position, they would retire to another farther up the ridge and equally difficult to take. It was impossible to flank their positions on account of the impassable cañons on each side. The entire band of hostiles numbered more than 150 men and boys capable of bearing arms, all well armed with modern repeating rifles and plentifully supplied with cartridges. If a raiding band was pressed too closely by a superior force they would scatter like a flock of frightened quail through a mountain range two hundred miles long by one hundred wide with not a human habitation in it.

Defeat was the invariable portion for the Mexican troops, regulars or irregulars, who attempted to invade the Indian stronghold; and they had quit the game as not worth the candle, leaving the hostiles free to raid their own towns, New Mexico, and Arizona at their sweet wills. The Indians would frequently enter the Mexican towns, declare an armistice, and go on a high old drunk with the citizens to celebrate it. A month later they might be at war with that town and at peace with another not twenty miles away.

The threats of the territorial newspapers and the hostile attitude of the towns near the border were causing the General much anxiety. The Indians still in Mexico had promised to come out in about "two moons." They were to send word later just when they would reach the border. Two moons passed, and then three, with nothing being heard from them. The tension was growing greater and the General's anxiety increasing as the newspapers became more virulent in their attacks upon him and upon his policy. In October he ordered me to proceed to the border with one of my companies of scouts, get in touch with the hostiles if possible, and hurry up their move to the Reservation. As soon as they reached the border I was to push them through as fast as possible to San Carlos, giving them protection *en route*. I being a regular officer of the army and my scouts regularly enlisted soldiers, an attack on us would be an attack upon the forces of the Federal Government, at that time controlling the territories—a serious offense.

Company B was selected for this duty because it had been reorganized when the hostiles came up with the General; about a third of the company had been dismissed and their places filled by the enlistment of some of the Chiricahua and Warm Springs who had come in with the General. It was on these men we were depending to get in touch with the hostiles still out.

But one untoward incident marked our trip to the border—an incident that affected me only, but which kept me in a nervous state for a month or more and gives me a creepy feeling when I think of it even to this day. One afternoon a hard rain came up that lasted well into the night. One of my scouts was an old medicine man, highly esteemed by all the Indians regardless of tribal relations. He had only the usual scant clothing of the Indians and becoming chilled by the cold rain asked me to lend him my saddle blanket for additional covering during the night. We camped at San Bernardino Springs, on the border of Arizona and Sonora. A few days later I began to break out in red pimples that itched like a rash and would not let me sleep. I stood it for several days, then called my pack master, Bill Duclin, into consultation.

Bill made an examination, then stepped away with the exclamation:

"Good Lord, Lieutenant, don't come near me!"

"What's the matter, Bill?" I asked in alarm, "have I got something catching?"

"Hell, no," Bill replied, "you've got something to catch! Lieutenant, you're lousy!"

Bill evidently was experienced. Under his tutelage every scrap of clothing I had with me, and my bedding and saddle blankets were taken down to the springs and dumped into the water, where they remained all that night; Bill, after seeing me thoroughly washed and disinfected with some tar soap kept to wash sores on the mules' backs, kindly let me have some pack-train blankets to sleep in. A week later the process was repeated, then I registered a solemn oath to shoot any Indian, medicinally inclined or not, who ever again asked the loan of my saddle blankets, even to protect him from a hurricane of hailstones.

A half-day's ride to the east was Animas Valley teeming with antelope; the intervening hills furnished deer, white-tail or black at your choice; Cajon Bonita (called by the whites, Skeleton Cañon) just on the Mexican border, offered turkeys for the taking. All these backed by an abundant and wholesome government ration manipulated by José Maria Soto, a camp cook from dreamland! Don't you wish you had been there?

Half a mile south of our camp, in the brush that lined the little stream fed by the springs, there were hundreds of peccaries (small wild hogs) that offered excellent practice in snap shooting with a rifle. The clumps of bushes were from four or five to twenty or thirty feet apart, and the speed with which a hog would cross such space was something to marvel at. A rustle of dry leaves, a grunt, a streak of gray, and your bullet would hit the ground ten feet behind him. At the expense of half a hundred rounds of ammunition and many fruitless hours I succeeded in bagging several; but finding their meat tough and unpalatable I contented myself with the skins, to be sent to the folk back home. Tanned, they made unique floor mats.

Three of the scouts were sent into Mexico as far as they dared go for fear of encountering Mexican troops, but they failed to meet with any of the hostiles. Several weeks of weary waiting followed, then one afternoon Nachite and Zele rode into our camp with about a dozen of their warriors and twice that number of women and children. They were well supplied with Mexican ponies and we made quick time to San Carlos, meeting no opposition *en route.*

When these people and the bands that followed them came out of Mexico they were the most perfect specimens of the racing type of athlete that one could wish to see. With the exception of Nachite, six feet one in his moccasins, they were of medium height, few over five feet eight, but proportioned like deer. Small hands and feet; small bones; thin arms and legs, the latter sinewed as though with steel cords, so taut were the sinews and devoid of fat. Chests broad, deep, and full, the heritage from generations of mountain-dwelling ancestors, they moved along the trail with a smooth, effortless stride that seemed as tireless as a machine and as rhythmical. The thought of attempting to catch one of them in the mountains gave me a queer feeling of helplessness, but I enjoyed a sensation of the beautiful in watching them.

A return to San Bernardino and several more weeks of waiting; then Chato and Mangus with a band of fifty or sixty appeared, also well mounted, and with little impedimenta. We again traveled fast and without incident. When Chato had reached our camp at the Springs he decided to celebrate the event by killing a fine young Mexican mare among the stolen ponies he had brought with him. Through Mickey Free, he explained that he was killing the mare in my honor; much as Mexican bull-fighters kill a bull in honor of some patron of the Fiesta—an honor that usually costs the unlucky recipient fifty or a hundred dollars in presents to the matador and his gang of highwaymen.

With Chato, my acceptance of the honor was to consist only in consuming with him a choice portion of the meat. But after I had witnessed the struggles of the beautiful creature as he roped it and cut its throat, I had no heart for the feast and lost caste with him by my squeamishness.

As we neared Sulphur Springs on our way to the Reservation, I saw a young woman and an old one suddenly leave the column and start off on a tangent to the line of march. Calling one of the Indian sergeants I asked why they had left us. He laughed and answered in pigeon English:

"By-em-by baby."

And "by-em-by baby" it proved to be. At sundown the two came into camp at Sulphur Springs, the young woman with a newborn baby in her arms. We had marched thirty-five miles that day and she was riding astride. Thirty to forty miles daily for several days thereafter was our stint, but she asked no favors.

Chapter VI

Geronimo arrives. Problem of cattle. Demands of United States Marshal and Collector of Customs.

HAVING delivered Chato's party to Crawford, I returned to the border to await Geronimo, of whom we had had no news. A dreary wait of six weeks followed with no sign of him. My scouts, now almost all Chiricahua and Warm Springs, became impatient. The services of my old friend, the medicine man, were called for to determine where Geronimo was and when he would appear.

Preparations for the offices of the Reverend Doctor were elaborate. First a brush hut was built on a plot of ground a little remote from the camp, so he might be undisturbed. The hut was covered with canvas from the pack trains, only a small opening being left. With his pouch of "medicine" the Doctor entered the hut and the opening was closed.

There he remained all that day and into the night, uttering incantations and from time to time burning a pungent powder, the odor of which we could smell a dozen yards away. Toward nine or ten o'clock he came out of the hut; but the incantations were not yet finished. From his right hand depended a thin buckskin thong to the end of which was attached a small, flat piece of wood with a hole in it. Twirling this around his head it gave out a shrill, whistling noise, not unlike the call of a night-bird.

Around and around his hut he went, then around the camp and through it, north to south, east to west, swinging his call and uttering incantations. The scouts, squatting in a circle, awaited his decision. The camp and all points of the compass properly incanted, he stopped at the scouts' camp fire, threw on it his pungent powder, and raising his face to the stars in a singsong chant made many gestures with his waving arms; then suddenly he ceased and, bathed in sweat, tottering a little with weakness, announced that he had found Geronimo.

Entering the circle of the scouts, he prolonged the suspense for several minutes while he gazed at the stars and mumbled a final incantation. Then he announced that Geronimo was three days away, riding on a white mule, and bringing a great lot of horses.

I was sending daily three or four scouts to patrol south and west along the border as we were not sure at just what point Geronimo might come in. Some four or five days after the Reverend Doctor's prophecy the patrol came in with the report that Geronimo was nearing the border and would arrive that afternoon; also, that he was riding a white pony.

How did the medicine man come so close to it? A signal from Geronimo's party? Not likely, as the Doctor was of the Tonto-Mohave tribe, bitter enemies of the Chiricahua. Had there been any signaling between the scouts and Geronimo's band the signals would have been known to the scouts, some of whom had relatives with Geronimo.

In addition to my company of scouts, recruited almost wholly from the Chiricahua and Warm Springs who had previously come in, I had with me a pack train of forty packs, fifteen saddle mules, eleven packers, mostly Mexican, and a cavalryman for courier in case of need.

It was not long before I was praying that the whole outfit might sprout wings.

There was also in my camp at this time a civilian, who represented himself as a writer gathering material for stories of the Indians. He left as soon as the patrol reported that Geronimo was coming, but I had reason to remember him later.

The only livestock Zele and Chato had brought with them were ponies, a hundred or so with each band and stolen, of course, from the Mexican ranches below the border. Geronimo was more provident.

As I sat on my mule at the international line watching the Indians coming up through the valley, I was surprised to see a great cloud of dust following them at an interval of two or three miles. My first thought was of a large force of Mexican troops in pursuit. But the Indians in advance, now plainly visible, showed no signs of haste or excitement.

In a few minutes Geronimo and fifteen or sixteen of his men and some seventy women and children arrived at the line. I had sent two of my scouts to meet them below the line and explain who we were and our reason for being there; a necessary precaution, taken also with Zele and Chato, as the Indians were as wary and suspicious as so many wild animals.

Riding up to me and checking his pony only when its shoulder had bumped the shoulder of my mule, his first words were an angry demand to know why there was need of an escort for him and his people to the Reservation. He had made peace with the Americans, why then was there danger of their attacking him?

I explained that there were some bad Americans just as there were some bad Indians and that on passing near a town some of these bad men, full of whiskey, might try to cause trouble. That the scouts were now American soldiers and if an American killed one of them the man would himself be hanged by the Americans. This satisfied him; he shook hands with me and assured me that he and I were thenceforth brothers.

That settled, I called his attention to the cloud of dust that was slowly approaching.

"Ganado," he explained, laconically, in Spanish.

And cattle they were, 350 head of beeves, cows, and half-grown calves stolen from the Mexican ranches just below the international line.

My heart beats went up to a record!

On my two previous trips to the Reservation I had avoided attack from the excited citizens of the southern Arizona towns by rapid marches of forty or fifty miles daily, keeping away from the traveled routes and attracting the least attention possible from any ranches near which we had to pass. We made the 175 miles to the Reservation in four or five days. But with this herd of slow-moving cattle, at their normal gait of twelve or fifteen miles daily it would take us two weeks. And instead of avoiding the ranches and traveled roads we would have to seek them for water and easier going for the cattle. Any attempt to drive them over the rocky hills and gulches of our former routes would result in many becoming footsore in three or four days, necessitating their abandonment—to which Geronimo would assuredly object.

To add to my woes, Geronimo's next demand was for a three-day halt then and there to rest the cattle in the luxuriant grass of the valley, explaining that they had been driven hard for fear of pursuit by the Mexican owners.

More time for the enraged citizens to organize and put their threats into execution! I vetoed the proposal emphatically and compromised on a start the following afternoon.

Two nights later I had just turned into my blankets when suddenly from the direction of my scouts' camp, a hundred yards away, there came a succession of wild yells, followed by several shots fired in rapid succession. I tumbled out of bed and raced to the camp through the rocks and thorns, unmindful, in the excitement, of my bare feet. Arriving there I found one of my scouts, a Tonto and a bitter enemy of the Chiricahua, parading up and down the camp cursing the whole race of Chiricahua and daring them to send out the best man among them to fight him. His remarks he was punctuating with alternating explosions of yells and cartridges. Neither the scouts nor the Chiricahua were paying any attention to him, but he was having a glorious time by himself. Some scoundrel had sold him a bottle of whiskey.

I sent for the first sergeant of the scouts, whose only comment was:

"He no do nothin'."

But fearing that the example might become contagious, I disarmed him and tied him to a tree, where he made music for the camp till exhausted. The next morning he was sober and sorry.

The route I selected to get Geronimo and his cattle to the Reservation was via Sulphur Springs Ranch, a small cattle ranch thirty miles west of Fort Bowie. Among the officers at Fort Bowie was a fellow Texan and West Point chum, Lieutenant J. Y. F. Blake, later known to history as Colonel Blake of the Irish Brigade in the Boer War. I need hardly add that he was Irish, with an Irish heart and an Irishman's love for a scrap.

After my two previous trips to the Reservation, Blake had written me deploring my unfriendliness in not giving him a chance to spend a night with me for old times' sake; and now, especially, as he had once been in a scrap with Geronimo's band and was anxious to know what they looked like. When I decided to camp at Sulphur Springs, I sent him a note advising him the night I would be there.

We were traveling only eighteen or twenty miles a day, less than half the distance I had covered daily on my two previous trips, but Geronimo was not satisfied. Every night he would come to my tent with a protest against such long marches—we were "running all the fat off the cattle and they would not be fit for trading when we reached the Reservation."

On one pretext or another I managed to pacify him until the night before we were to reach Sulphur Springs, an old Indian camping ground noted for its fine water and grass. He announced his ultimatum—I could go to Hades with my scouts and pack train, he was going to lie over at Sulphur Springs two or three days to give his cattle a rest.

I had been holding in reserve one argument for just such an emergency and I now sprang it on him. He had seen General Crook in Mexico with American troops. The Mexicans had the same right to come into the United States. We were too near the border to risk stopping, as the Mexicans might be following us.

"Mexicans!" he snarled, "Mexicans! My squaws can whip all the Mexicans in Chihuahua."

"But the Mexicans have plenty of cartridges and you have practically none," I argued, as I pointed to his nearly empty cartridge belt.

"We don't fight Mexicans with cartridges," he replied contemptuously. "Cartridges cost too much. We keep them to fight your white soldiers. We fight Mexicans with rocks."

I capitulated and compromised on a halt for one day when we reached the Springs. But "the best laid plans of mice and men."

I wish to emphasize this picture of Sulphur Springs Ranch, and especially the topography of the country around it. The ranch house was a one-story adobe building surrounded by an adobe wall four or five feet high enclosing a couple of acres of ground and the springs. This wall on its northerly side passed within ten feet of the house and at that point contained a small gate. In every direction from the ranch stretched the unbroken prairie lands of Sulphur Springs Valley, as level almost as a billiard table and destitute of trees or brush higher than a man's waist. At this time of the year, the time of drouth in the Southwest, the dust raised by grazing cattle could be seen for many miles, the vegetation hardly affording cover for a squirrel.

The pack train went into camp about fifty yards from the small gate, the scouts a little farther out. There was a light breeze blowing and a twinge of chill in the air that induced several of the hostile families to select as a camping place the lee side of the adobe wall, two of them with their children and household belongings on either side of the gate. The other families scattered about the ranch at points convenient to water.

The cattle, mules, and ponies, after watering, were

grazing half a mile away, where the grass was better than near the ranch; three mounted Indians were on herd to keep the cattle from mixing with the cattle of the ranch.

I had just finished pitching my tent and was waiting for the cook's call to supper when two men in civilian clothes came out of the ranch house and approached my tent. As they came toward me I had time to note from their dress and the pallor of their faces that they were evidently city dwellers. Some chance travelers, I thought, or friends of the ranch owner, who wanted a closer glimpse of real, live, wild Apache.

They introduced themselves as—well, Jones and Smith—I have forgotten their names.

They evinced great interest in me and in my charges, and asked many questions; not impertinently, just casually. Such questions as any polite but curious person might ask. Thus they got out of me my name and rank, the number of men in Geronimo's party, how many scouts I had, how many civilian packers, and finally the approximate number of ponies and cattle Geronimo had brought with him.

Then they exploded their bombs!

One of them drew back the lapel of his coat and displaying his badge informed me that he was the United States Marshal for the Southern District of Arizona. His companion chipped in as the Collector of Customs from Nogales, the Arizona port of entry from Mexico.

I jumped to the conclusion that some one of my packers had got mixed up in some smuggling scrape and was wanted for it.

"No," replied the Marshal, "we don't want your packers. These cattle and ponies that Geronimo has brought in are contraband. In the eyes of the law they are smuggled. Moreover, Geronimo and his men are wanted for the murder of Arizona citizens. I order you to arrest them and take them with their smuggled stock to Tucson for trial."

I replied that I would not attempt to obey such an order unless it came from General Crook himself and asked the Marshal if he had such an order.

He had not, but reaching into his pocket he took out a paper, scribbled a few words on it and handed it to me with the remark that he thereby subpoenaed me as a citizen of the United States to aid in the arrest of the Indians.

"And," he added, "tomorrow morning I am going to subpoena as well your civilian packers, and the five cowboys at the ranch. If you and your packers still refuse to aid me, I am going to Willcox and organize a posse with every available man in the town. I am going to have those Indians and then I am going to see that you answer to the Federal courts for your refusal to obey my order."

Willcox was a small village and railroad station about forty miles north of Sulphur Springs and some half a dozen miles off the route I had in mind for our trek to the Reservation. At most it could furnish a dozen or fifteen men.

I tried to persuade him not to make the attempt. I pointed out that of my thirty-three scouts all but eight or ten were Chiricahua themselves, the "uncles and the cousins and the aunts" of Geronimo's twenty-six warriors; that of my eleven packers, most of them Mexicans, only four were armed with rifles, some not armed at all; that even with the addition of the citizens from Willcox we would be outnumbered nearly three to one by the most determined and skilful guerrilla fighters in the West. We might make a few "good Indians" but it was morally certain that few of us would be left to boast of it.

The Marshal was obdurate. It was his duty and he was going to perform it, no matter what the consequences. In the morning he would subpoena my packers.

"No hard feelings, Lieutenant," he said, as he and the Collector started back to the ranch house. "You must do your duty as you see it and I must do mine. But remember that you as a citizen are now under my orders until I need you tomorrow."

A pretty kettle of fish!

If I obeyed the Marshal and attempted to arrest Geronimo and his band the best I could hope for was to pass in my checks with the men of my race. If by chance I survived I would have failed in the duty General Crook had entrusted to me and would be deservedly kicked out of the army.

If I defied the Marshal, as I determined to do, and he organized his posse, I wondered who would kill me, the posse or the Indians. There seemed to be little preference. If by any chance I escaped both, and the citizens of Arizona didn't lynch me, there was the Federal court and jail in the background.

I was too far from Fort Bowie, the nearest military post, to get help or advice from there. I thought of warning Geronimo at once. But he was already angry and rebellious over the treatment of his cattle and the suggestion of danger from the citizens of Arizona. To tell him now that this danger was at hand would be tantamount to starting him and nearly all of my scouts instantly back for the border less than fifty miles away, with the certainty that many of the Chiricahua recently taken to the Reservation would break out again to rejoin their relatives in Mexico, leaving the usual red trail of blood and fire in their wake.

My orders from the General were to see that Geronimo and his people got *safely* to the Reservation. If the Marshal persisted in his determination I might not get all the Indians safely to the Reservation, but I believed they would stick with me if I stuck with them.

By the time the Marshal could organize his posse and attack us we would be two days farther from the border and that much nearer the reservation line. If we were attacked, the pack train with the women and children could continue their flight to the Reservation, while I with my scouts and Geronimo's men stood off the Marshal and his posse.

I had promised Geronimo that we would lie over a day at Sulphur Springs, a promise that had now to be broken. What excuse could I give him without telling him facts that would send him scurrying back to Mexico? I was struggling with this problem when a scout on guard called out that a small cloud of dust was approaching from the direction of Fort Bowie.

"Bo" Blake!

Not a chance in the world that it could be anyone else on that lonely road with the Apache known to be out. In my excitement I had forgotten my note to him.

As I stood near my tent, eagerly waiting to see if my surmise was true, a plan for escape from my predicament suddenly suggested itself. Blake's coming was like a flash of lightning that shows the path on a pitch-dark night. When he dismounted at my tent I was feeling almost cheerful.

To carry out what I had in mind, I had to have Geronimo's coöperation, which I was not at all certain to get in *his* frame of mind.

The plan looked simple. So does flying.

Blake had graduated a year ahead of me at West Point and so was technically my superior officer. He was to take command and order me to remain at the Springs, subject to the Marshal's orders, while he with the pack train, the Indians, and their live stock "lit out" for the Reservation as soon as the Marshal and the cowboys were safely asleep.

What would happen if the people in the ranch house were awakened by the noise of breaking camp? That they would start immediately for Willcox to raise a posse that night and pursue the Indians the next day, was the probability.

Other difficulties presented themselves. When Crawford, Gatewood, and I were detached from our regiments and placed in control of the San Carlos Reservation we were put on General Crook's staff, receiving orders only from him. Other officers in the Department, regardless of their rank, had been told it was "hands off" where we were concerned. Moreover, Blake had permission to be away from his post for only one night. He would be lucky if he got back in a week. But he was game and I was desperate.

We left the tent to give Blake a chance to look over the disposition of the camp before dark.

"Good Lord!" he exclaimed, as he saw the job we had before us. "Pack up and move those bellowing mules right under the noses of those cowboys! And look at those Indians camped against that 'dobe wall, where the Marshal could reach out his hand and grab them. There ain't a chance in a thousand of our getting away without a fight. Well, if he starts it he'll have to have it."

I had a plan for moving the pack train and felt that the Indians would be equal to their task if I could talk Geronimo into a reasonable frame of mind and prevent him from flying off the handle when I suggested flight to the Reservation.

Blake and I had just finished supper and were lolling in front of the cook's fire when the Marshal and the Collector suddenly joined us. My heart went down into my boots. What if they had come to subpoena Blake? But my luck was back on duty again. They had come only for a friendly chat and, it developed later, to crow over me a little.

I introduced Blake as a West Point chum who had come out to spend the night with me for old times' sake. Blake was the beau ideal of a soldier; tall, handsome, straight as an arrow, with a warm, magnetic personality that gripped you instantly.

He had brought with him a quart of good Scotch whiskey. We had had a bracer each before supper but the bottle was still practically full and Blake produced it.

"Say, this Arizona of yours is sure one damn dry country," was his explanation, "don't you fellows want a drink?"

I could almost see their mouths water at the suggestion. They said that they had been there three days waiting for me, had exhausted their liquor, and "sure were thirsty." For an hour they stayed with us. Blake was a generous host and our guests got the lion's share of that

Scotch, Blake swearing that he had another bottle; but when they left they carried within them the last drop of the only bottle he had.

"We can send old Geronimo in to scalp that pair tonight without their waking up," laughed Blake as we watched them on their way back to the ranch house.

During their visit the Marshal had a good laugh at my expense as he related how he had "put one over on me."

"Lieutenant," he asked, "while you were down on the border did you see anything of a writer who was looking for Indian stories?"

I replied that such a man had been in my camp several times.

"Writer!" chuckled the Marshal. "What he writes is what brought me here. You beat me out on your two other trips up because you moved so fast I did not get word in time to head you off. But you can't drive cattle like you can ponies."

By ten o'clock the camp was as quiet as a church. An occasional jingle of the bell on the pack train lead horse as he shook off a mosquito or scratched a bite, and the croaking of the frogs at the springs were the only distinguishable sounds that broke the stillness.

I walked down to the gate at the ranch house and listened. I could hear only the heavy breathing of tired men. But what I *saw* gave me a jolt. The Marshal or the Collector, I could not tell which, had brought his bedding out of the room they occupied and was asleep on the porch. Standing there at the gate between the two sleeping Indian families, I could almost reach out my hand and touch that unconscious form. But evidently

Blake had done good work. Their breathing was like the exhaust of an aeroplane.

Returning to the camp, I sent for my Indian first sergeant, told him I was going to move camp at once, and wanted his assistance in persuading Geronimo to listen to reason. He asked for no explanation but said simply that what I ordered would be carried out. I then sent for Geronimo.

After a little time he appeared, and with him several of his men, all armed. Their cartridge belts that a few hours before were nearly empty of cartridges were now filled to the last notch. Half of my scout company had sprung up, it seemed to me, out of the ground and were silently waiting for orders.

I had decided to tell Geronimo neither the whole truth nor the exact truth; either would have sent him scurrying back to Mexico if the scouts did not kill him in the attempt. I did not know what my scout sergeant had in mind, but I did know that he was of a tribe hostile to the Chiricahua and that he hated Geronimo from the depths of his soul.

I told Geronimo that the two men he had seen talking to me in the afternoon were civilian officers of the Government in Washington. That when anyone brought cattle into the United States they had to pay for them and these officers were there to collect the money. That the charge on his cattle was about a thousand dollars, which the Collector demanded that I pay, or that I take the cattle to Tucson for sale.

That I had refused to do either and they intended to take the cattle from us in the morning and send them to Tucson with the cowboys at the ranch. To this I knew he, Geronimo, would not consent, and to avoid trouble we had better start for the Reservation immediately and get so far on the road by morning that pursuit would be useless. My brother (Blake) would go with him and I would remain at the ranch to throw the officers off the trail if they tried to follow him.

As I talked to him he stood staring me straight in the eyes, his anger mounting and his lips twitching as he shifted his rifle from arm to arm. My sergeant was standing silently beside him, the other scouts and Geronimo's men forming a circle around us; Blake, with his pistol drawn but concealed under his coat, was backing me up. The whole group tense and waiting.

As I expected, Geronimo's answer was an angry and emphatic "No!" Then he went on to say that he had come in for peace but had found only trouble and threats. He was tired of it. If these men thought that they could take his cattle away from him, let them try it tomorrow. He was going back to bed and would hold me to my promise of a lay-over right where we were. Then he contemptously demanded to know why I had disturbed him for a trivial talk that meant nothing.

Here my Indian sergeant took a hand and words shot from him like the rattle of a machine gun in action as he faced Geronimo. What he said I never knew. The moment was too tense for Mickey Free to interrupt and interpret.

Geronimo's feathers began to droop. He glanced at his men and at the scouts. Nothing in them seemed to encourage him. After one or two ineffectual attempts to break in on the sergeant with arguments of his own, he confined himself to grunts and monosyllables. I saw that he was weakening and suggested that probably he was afraid his people were not smart enough to get away without the men in the ranch knowing it.

This touched him in a tender spot and he instantly resented it. "His people could leave me standing where I was and I would not know that they were gone." I followed up my advantage by pointing out what a joke it would be on the officers in the ranch if they woke up in the morning and found that the Indians with all the cattle and ponies had disappeared.

Geronimo almost smiled, hesitated for a moment, looked inquiringly at his men, saw no opposition from them, and the battle was won.

I went at once to the pack train, woke the pack master, and hurriedly explained the situation. With the assistance of the scouts the *aparejos* (enormous packsaddles made of heavy leather and stuffed with straw) were carried four or five hundred yards from camp, where the mules could be saddled without danger of disturbing the people in the ranch. Fortunately we had about exhausted our grain for the mules and rations for the men, so had little cargo to move.

A handkerchief stuffed in the bell on the lead horse silenced it. The horse was white and the mules could follow him readily, no matter how dark the night. They were old campaigners, accustomed to sudden moves, and no trouble would be had with them in packing up. Leaving these matters to the pack master, I went to resume my station at the gate of the ranch house and await eventualities.

When I reached the gate there were no Indians there and none along the adobe fence. From the ranch house there still came only that chorus of deep, heavy breathing, every breath of it carrying up to Heaven from me a prayer that it would continue until morning. From the direction of the camp the only sound that reached me was the croaking of the frogs at the springs—"They're on the run—on the run—on the run."

After half an hour I returned to the camp. The only things in sight were my saddle mule tied to a stake near the embers of the cook's fire, and an empty box which the pack master had considerately left for a seat during my long night's vigil.

The sun was above the horizon before there was any sign of life in the ranch house. Then the form on the porch moved, sat up, stretched, looked about, and began a yawn that died a-borning as he scrambled to his feet and ran to the gate. I saw that it was the Collector.

In about three jumps he was back and through the door of his room yelling:

"They're gone! They're gone!"

In a moment he was out again with the Marshal, sleepily rubbing his eyes. The Marshal looked, but what he saw was not enough. Back he ran into his room and reappeared with a pair of field glasses.

Against the side of the house was a ladder that gave access to the roof. Up this the Marshal and Collector climbed, painfully I thought and hoped, in their "undies" and bare feet.

For several minutes they stood on the roof searching with their glasses every point of the horizon. Certainly five hundred cattle, mules, and ponies could not conceal their movements on that dusty plain if anywhere within twenty miles of the ranch. But the only things in sight were the ranch cattle coming in to water and a dejected-looking second lieutenant seated on a cracker box holding a sleepy-looking mule by the bridle.

Slowly they climbed down the ladder and reëntered their room. In a few minutes they came out again fully dressed and walked over to where I was awaiting them.

"Where are those Indians?" asked the Marshal.

"They're gone," I answered rather inanely.

"Cut out your impertinence and answer my question," he demanded, "can't I see they're gone? What I want to know is, where they are gone."

"That I can't tell you," I replied. "The officer I introduced to you last night is my superior. When I reported to him the condition of things he took the command away from me, ordered me to remain here in obedience to your subpoena, and left with the outfit about ten o'clock last night, ten hours ago. By now they must be forty miles from here. But whether they went toward Fort Bowie, or toward Fort Grant, or Geronimo lit out for Mexico as he threatened to do and Blake followed him, I don't know. Blake did not tell me his plans and it would have been an impertinence for me, his junior, to have questioned him."

The Marshal looked me straight in the eyes.

"You are lying," he said.

"Perhaps I am, but you can't prove it," I replied with a smile, the first time I had felt like smiling in several days.

He and the Collector held a council of war over the chance of catching Blake. If Blake had gone south, east, or north, with a ten hours' start he would be at the border, at Fort Bowie or near Camp Grant, just north of Willcox, where there were several companies of soldiers stationed, before the Marshal could possibly organize a posse and overtake him. Certainly he had not gone west. In that direction lay Tucson.

"Well," decided the Marshal finally, "I guess we are beat and may as well go home."

The Collector agreed.

I then reminded the Marshal that I was there in obedience to his orders. If he had no further need of me I would like to go back to my post at San Carlos.

"You can go to hell as far as I am concerned, and I wish you a happy journey," he concluded forcefully but not unpleasantly as he and the Collector turned to face the grinning cowboys, now peering over the adobe wall.

A few steps away they turned back and shook hands with me.

"It was a mighty slick trick, Lieutenant," were the Marshal's parting words, "but I would never have believed it possible if I had not seen it. The Collector and I slept like logs, but those cow-punchers are supposed to sleep with one eye open."

After two days of hard riding I overtook Blake a few miles south of the reservation line and we delivered our charges to Crawford at San Carlos without further incident.

Geronimo's theft of the cattle profited him little. They were taken from him and turned in to the Agency for beef, the Mexican owners being later compensated by our Government.

The loss of his prized possessions, after all he had gone through to obtain and preserve them, became a thorn in Geronimo's side and one of the main factors in the outbreak a year later, when with 143 of the 550 Chiricahua under my charge near Fort Apache he left the Reservation and made history in the Southwest by what has become known as the Geronimo campaign.

Chapter VII

Hostiles select Turkey Creek as a home. A mistake in policy. They receive wagons and farm implements. Efforts to use them. Crossing of Black River. Turkey Creek a paradise. A bear episode. Some Indian history. Tizwin. Dutchy. Two sides to a story.

WITH every man, woman, and child of the hostiles back on the Reservation, the General permitted them to select the part of it they desired for their home. They selected the vicinity of Turkey Creek, a small stream seventeen miles southwest of Fort Apache and near that portion of the Reservation occupied by the White Mountain bands, to whom several of the hostiles were related by marriage or otherwise.

Crawford and I favored establishing them as a pastoral rather than as an agricultural people. Turkey Creek had no water for agricultural purposes, nor was there any vacant land near Fort Apache suitable to sustain any large number of them. Nomads for generations past, their natural bent was the acquisition and care of animals. We proposed that they be given sheep and a few cows to start with, hoping that in time they would become independent, peaceful, and prosperous as the Navaho. I believe the General would have accepted our view, but the Indian Bureau at Washington was again in the saddle and farmers they must be.

Recent press dispatches inform me that this idea of furnishing the Apache with sheep as a means to their becoming self-supporting, is being tried out with much success among the Mescalero and Jicarillo Apache of the Mescalero Agency in New Mexico.

My charges were given a dozen light wagons with a set of double harness for each; a dozen plows; two dozen or so picks and shovels; a few bags of corn and wheat for seed, and about the first of June were told to be on their way, with me in command of the hejira. Then the fun began. The Indians' ponies would weigh some seven to eight hundred pounds; the harnesses sent them were for horses double that size. Crawford, West, Elliott, and I laughed till we ached over the efforts of the Indians to harness their ponies in harnesses big enough for two of them. None of the ponies had ever before seen such a thing as a wagon or a harness; many of them had never even been broken to saddle. I honestly believe that some of them could have crawled through the collars put on them if given a little time.

By stuffing the collars with anything available in the way of old rags, cutting the harness to shreds, and the assistance of half a dozen Indians to each pony, a wagon would finally be hitched up, the proud proprietor would mount it, seize the reins, and away he would go over the plain at full tilt, his erstwhile assistants scrambling into the tail end of the wagon as it passed them on the run. The Indians, whooping and laughing, were getting as much fun out of the circus as we were.

Later some of them tried out their new plows in the San Carlos river bottom. The ponies, unaccustomed to a slow gait, preferred to trot or gallop, and the plow-points were oftener above ground than in it. Now and then a point would strike a hidden root or stump; then the plowman would execute a somersault over the plow handles, to the great delight of his friends. A furrow, when completed, had the regularity of the trail of a snail on a bat.

We had had two weeks of such preparation before Crawford deemed it safe to let us set out. Unfortunately, the movies had not then been invented. What a picture that migration would have made! And our crossing of Black River! Nothing else like it has ever been seen.

Black River, immortalized by Pat Keogh, was in flood when we arrived at its banks. A small, dilapidated old ferry boat lay water-logged near midstream. To rescue it, bail it out, patch up its leaks, and ferry my party across would take a week or more. The General with his staff and escort was only two days behind me, coming up from San Carlos to see the Indians located in their new home. Something had to be done.

In my duck hunting, boyhood days I had used a canvas boat; a mere wooden frame covered with canvas but very serviceable. In the pack trains we had some large sheets of canvas for the protection of the cargo in case of rain. The bodies of the Indian wagons were light. A canvas was stretched on the ground, a wagon body set on it, the canvas folded over the sides of the wagon body and made fast, and a boat was ready. Four such boats were prepared.

Just below the ferry crossing, the river made a sharp bend, eddying back on its course; but the current was so swift that to take our improvised boats straight across it would have swamped them, had we tried to pull them across hand over hand on a rope stretched from bank to bank. A number of pack train ropes were tied together and an end fastened to a tree on our side of the river. An Indian swam across with the other end, took in all the slack, and tied it to a tree a little distance downstream. Swimming back to our side and again downstream, the rope was made fast, then the end carried up to the tree where our first tie was made. By thus taking advantage of the eddy we had a downstream haul for our boats over and back—a water merry-go-round. A party of passengers with their belongings would be loaded at point number one, scooted on an angle downstream to point number two, unloaded, the boat hauled downstream along the river bank to point number three, scooted across, again downstream, to point number four and back over the eddying water along the bank on our side to the point of embarkation. The Indians fell for the scheme with the greatest glee and almost fought for the fun of being boatman. Wagon gears were pulled across through the water by ponies hitched to ropes, the mules and horses swam, and by noon of the second day after our arrival at the river we were all across and most of the Indians at Turkey Creek.

The packers, meantime, had resurrected the ferry boat and had it ready for the General and his party when they arrived that night. I had waited for the General and had a little fun with him for a few minutes while I let him think we had all crossed in the dinky little ferry that would not accommodate half a dozen horses at a time. As the Indians had over three hundred horses and my pack trains nearly a hundred mules, to say nothing of the Indians' wagons, personal effects, families, and my two pack trains of supplies, the crossing in a day and a half looked nothing short of a miracle. A miracle it would have been to have crossed that outfit by that ferry in a week. The General was greatly interested and not a little amused when I explained the engineering feat.

The Indians, when we left San Carlos, numbered 512. On our arrival at Turkey Creek members of the Coyotero tribe, a tribe closely affiliated with the Chiricahua, began to join them. Later some of the White Mountain did likewise, and in a month or two I had a few more than 550 Indians under my charge. Of these, 127 were Chiricahua and Warm Springs men and boys capable of bearing arms. Company B was still with me, but Chato had been made first sergeant and Juan, a half-brother to Geronimo, second sergeant. Geronimo's son, Chappo, demanded the post of striker (servant) to me, as it paid five dollars more per month than the pay of an ordinary scout. His activities reminded me of Tom Brown in his schooldays. The hardest work he did was saddling my mule, smoking my cigarettes, and loafing around Sam Bowman's cook tent.

Mickey Free as interpreter and Sam Bowman as cook and general camp helper completed my staff. These two, Mickey and Bowman, were the only men, barring Indians, with me during the ensuing eleven months in camp; and my only associates except on the rare occasions of a visit by an officer from Fort Apache or by West from San Carlos, events that could be counted on one hand in the six months I was at Turkey Creek.

Company B had been again reorganized and now consisted entirely of Chiricahua and Warm Springs selected from the recently hostile bands. Some of these scouts had never before been on a reservation; but when a crisis arose—there were several, two especially serious —they proved themselves thoroughly loyal, with a full sense of their duty and a determination to fulfil it at any cost to themselves.

Turkey Creek was a beauty spot and a game paradise. On the crest of a spur of the White Mountains, the climate in summer was ideal. My camp was pitched in a little glade on the stream of crystal-clear water. Surrounding the camp were giant pines, with low hills rising to the south and north. As we entered their domain, wild turkeys fled before us. The Indians reported deer and bears within an hour's ride. In shallow pools giant frogs croaked a welcome, oblivious of the doom I mentally promised them, a promise soon made good.

The Indians scattered among the trees and began erecting their simple homes of brush covered with cotton cloth, old shirts, pieces of blankets, or any other available material. This work fell to the women, the men starting gambling games or lolling in the shade of the trees as they criticized the work of the architects. Three of the scouts went out to hunt and in a couple of hours returned with a deer. A large hospital tent I had brought with me was erected near my own tent, a month's supply of rations stored in it, and the camp settled down for the summer.

The more suspicious and intractable of the Indians selected sites for their camps at a distance of several miles from mine. These were Mangus, Chihuahua, Geronimo, and their bands. The followers of Ka-ya-ten-nae did likewise; but he selected a site for himself on a ridge just above my camp, where he could see everything that went on in it.

By the time we were settled in camp and the excitement incident to establishing themselves in their new homes had worn off, it was past mid-June and the Indians claimed that it was too late to do any farming; the snow would soon come and kill the plants before corn could mature. Only those who had been given wagons and harnesses, and not all of these, seemed to feel any obligation to farm at all; but the majority promised to do great things in the spring.

Those big, fat frogs were a temptation, and their "jug-o-rum" war cry at night a defiance. I made a contract with two small Indians to pay five cents apiece for all the big ones they could catch for me, expecting that they might be able to get ten or a dozen at most, as the frogs had proved themselves too wary for my skill as a frog catcher. In two or three hours my contractors appeared with more frogs than both Bowman and I could have eaten in a week, and Bowman did not care for frogs. It nearly depleted the treasury to settle up and call the contract off. The small boys had shot the frogs with bow and arrow.

The morning after we made a camp a woman who must have been nearly sixty years of age came to me with a live, full grown turkey hen in her arms. She explained that she had run it down and caught it. As it seemed in perfect condition so far as we could tell after it was killed and dressed, I was disposed to doubt her feat; but the Indians asserted that she was telling the truth and that they frequently caught turkeys in that way for the fun of it. The Apache did not eat turkeys, claiming that they were not good to eat as turkeys ate snakes. That did not spoil my appetite for turkey. The woods were full of them and the young ones just right for a broil over a camp fire. Any day was Thanksgiving Day for us till we hungered for beef.

Small streams three or four miles to the south of our

camp were alive with mountain trout. There were literally thousands of them for every mile or two of creek. To me it was a wonder how they found food enough to exist. It was no trick at all to catch four or five dozen in four or five hours' fishing. They were small, seldom a pound in weight, but delicious eating. So ravenous were they that they would rise to any kind of bait—small frogs, worms, bugs, anything that looked like food. I had no artificial flies and frequently, when out of bait, would get them with a small green leaf, or a speck of the red flannel that had been scorned by the frogs.

I wrote such glowing tales of my surroundings to Crawford and West at San Carlos that they got the fever. Crawford could not leave, but most of his adored Troop F could. He sent about thirty of them up in command of West and they spent two weeks with me, having the time of their lives. West made them bring their daily catches of trout to him to count and when they left he told me the count was well up in the thousands. This did not start out to be a fish story, but since it has developed into one I am going to stake my reputation on it. I may say, however, that the fish, dressed and with their heads off, weighed but five or six ounces and it took quite a few to fill a robust, hungry man. The men ate all they could, then salted and dried on stake ropes stretched from tree to tree enough to fill two cook boxes. Some of these we had for Christmas dinner at San Carlos.

On this trip a hunting incident occurred that for sheer luck I have never seen equaled. A recruit in the troop decided he would go deer hunting. He returned a few hours later with this report:

Walking through the pine timber looking for a deer, he came upon a giant pine that had fallen to the ground, leaving its roots sticking up high in the air. He stepped upon a branch near the top of the tree and walked toward the root end, looking ahead for signs of deer. Near the root end he jumped down to the ground. As he did so a she bear that with her cub was making her home under the roots of the pine rose up and struck at him. She cut his blouse from just below the shoulder to below the waist, but did not so much as scratch him. He had his rifle in his hand ready cocked for a deer, and pushing the muzzle at her face without taking aim, he pulled the trigger. The bullet hit her squarely between the eyes, killing her instantly. He then reloaded and killed the cub, which made no attempt to attack him.

The men gave him a great "razz" by way of reward for such an improbable yarn, claiming that he had cut the blouse himself and would not be able to find the bears if a party went out with him. But he stuck to the story with so much earnestness that West was finally convinced there was something in it. A detail was sent out with him and we had bear meat for dinner. On its return, the detail reported conditions just as he had described them; and the face of the she bear was powder burned.

The Apache would kill a bear but would not touch it after killing it. They claimed that bears were the embodied spirits of men and women who had committed crimes while in this world and were suffering punishment for them. They could be put out of their misery but must not be touched for fear that the departing spirit might enter the body of the person touching them. On one occasion three of my scouts came upon five bears on the side of a cañon opposite to the side on which the scouts were, but within easy rifle range. They killed the five, then continued to shoot them till all the cartridges they had with them were exhausted. But I could not induce them to go back, skin the bears, and bring me the skins for a reward of five dollars to each man. As I was alone the skins were lost.

Living among these people with practically no companionship except that of the Indians themselves, my feelings toward them began to change. That ill-defined impression that they were something a little better than animals but not quite human; something to be on your guard against; something to be eternally watched with suspicion and killed with no more compunction than one would kill a coyote; the feeling that there could be no possible ground upon which we could meet as man to man, passed away.

The rank and file of the Indian men seldom came to my tent, but not a day would pass without one or more of the chiefs or principal men turning up for a talk and a smoke. Chato, my first sergeant, I of course saw daily to get his report on the general conditions in the camp and any needs of the scouts. From the older chiefs, Nana and Loco, I learned something of their tribal relations, which, for such value as it may have historically, I give here.

The earliest chiefs in their memory were Mangus Colorado, Cochise, and Delgadito. Mangus Colorado, they said, had been killed by the white men; Delgadito, in a fight with Mexicans; Cochise had died on a reservation near the Mexican border. After the deaths of Mangus Colorado and Delgadito there was only one big chief, Cochise. When he died, Victorio became chief of the Chiricahua and Loco actual chief of the Warm Springs, although Mangus Colorado's son, called Mangus after him, was entitled to the honor. Mangus was a quiet, peace-loving man with what would now be called an inferiority complex that unsuited him for the leadership of such warlike people.

With the death of Victorio at the hands of the Carrizal Mexicans and Mexican troops, Juh assumed the leadership, Nana being crippled by rheumatism. Juh met his death by drowning in the Casas Grandes River, near Casas Grandes, Chihuahua, while drunk. Geronimo claimed his place as leader of the Chiricahua bands; but being disliked by the majority of them, his following was confined to less than thirty men. Nachite, son of Cochise and the hereditary chieftain of the Chiricahua, was considered too frivolous for the post of leadership. After he joined Geronimo in the outbreak in 1885, however, he became one of the most determined, intractable, and defiant of the hostiles; more so than even Geronimo himself.

Loco, while generally acknowledged as chief of the Warm Springs, was, like Mangus, pacifically inclined, but he was a man of greater force and exercised a controlling influence over a considerable number of his people; an influence always in the paths of peace. Much against his advice and wishes he and they were forced off the San Carlos Reservation in the outbreak of May, 1882, when an armed band of Chiricahua came up from Mexico and demanded at the muzzles of their rifles that Loco and his people join them. Loco, like Nana, was growing old and could not at that time stem the tide of revolt. But when the outbreak of 1885 occurred his counsel prevailed and his people took no part in it. He had lost the use of one eye, over which a cataract had formed. This gave him a sinister appearance entirely foreign to his nature. He became my staunch friend and supporter in all questions that arose in my management of these Indians.

With no outstanding chief of the type of Mangus Colorado, Cochise, and Victorio, after the death of the latter, the Indians fell apart under several separate leaderships of subchiefs. The subchiefs were Chato, Zele, Benito, and Chihuahua, all of whom seemed to have some hereditary rank that I never clearly understood; possibly a rank that came down to them from the days when the tribe and the members of the various bands were far more numerous. Certain it is, however, that the rank and designation of these subchiefs was different from, and in a social sense superior to, that of Geronimo and Ka-ya-ten-nae, who had won their spurs in warfare, or by their skill as leaders of raids.

Geronimo was neither a chief nor a subchief. He had risen to the leadership of a faction (about one-fifth) of the warriors, by sheer courage, determination, and skill as a leader. But he was feared and disliked by the great majority of the Indians. This is shown conclusively by the facts that part of the Indians came in with the General, part under their chief Zele, accompanied by Nachite, and part under Chato. Later, immediately following the outbreak in 1885, Chihuahua with his people and Mangus with his, left Geronimo and Nachite. Still later, Chihuahua rejoined them, but because my scouts had captured most of his women and children and all his supplies and camp equipage, Mangus never rejoined them.

Like Geronimo, a much younger man, Ka-ya-ten-nae, about twenty-five years of age, had acquired leadership of a faction of the unruly and dissatisfied young men, thirty-two in number. His ambitions I nipped in the bud, narrowly escaping being nipped myself in doing it.

In my talks with the Indians they showed no resentment of the way they had been treated in the past; only wonderment at the why of it. Why had they been shifted from reservation to reservation; told to farm and had their crops destroyed; assured that the Government would ration them, then left to half starve; herded in the hot, malarial river bottoms of the Gila and San Carlos, when they were mountain people? These and other questions I could not answer. And above all they wondered if they would now be allowed to live at peace. Poor devils! Their fears were realized. In two years they were in prisons in Florida; four hundred innocent people, men, women, and children, who had kept the faith with us, punished for the guilt of barely one-fourth who had been lied to and frightened into leaving the Reservation by Geronimo, Chihuahua, and two or three other malcontents!

We have heard much talk of the treachery of the Indian. In treachery, broken pledges on the part of high officials, lies, thievery, slaughter of defenseless women and children, and every crime in the catalogue of man's inhumanity to man the Indian was a mere amateur compared to the "noble white man." His crimes were retail, ours wholesale. We learned his methods in that line and with our superior intelligence, improved upon them. The only thing we did not adopt was his method of torturing prisoners. We had better ones of our own in the prisons of our big cities; and our boasted civilization was little more than a hundred years away from the most exquisite torture ever devised by man—that of the Spanish Inquisition.

The attitude of the chiefs and subchiefs toward me, and other straws in the wind, soon showed that not all were content with their surrender. Chato, Benito, Zele, and Loco came frequently to my tent for friendly or business talks. The others held aloof. Nana, apparently over eighty years of age and crippled with rheumatism, might well be excused for sticking at home; but when the outbreak occurred the following year he rode horseback ninety miles without rest. But for the attitude of Geronimo, Nachite, Chihuahua, and Ka-ya-ten-nae I could assign no reason other than one of discontent and antagonism.

Geronimo never came to my tent unless he wanted something, and this in four months was not more than eight or ten times. I kept a stock of medicines on hand and an emergency kit for accidents. Twice he came for medicine. Nana, Chihuahua, and Ka-ya-ten-nae held aloof. Chihuahua came once, to protest against the General's edict that the making of tizwin must cease.

Tizwin was a crude beer made of corn, but with a strong alcoholic content. Drinking any quantity of it resulted in two things, a "bad Injun," and a hang-over for the next two or three days that made the Indian as tractable and companionable as a wounded bear. The General had given me orders to put a stop to its manufacture; first by persuasion, then by threats, and finally by putting offenders in the jail at Fort Apache. Chihuahua loved his toddy and entered a vigorous protest when the General's order was made known to him. That the General was entirely right in his effort to prohibit tizwin drinking was proved the following spring, when a tizwin drunk in defiance of this order was the culmination of dissatisfaction that finally caused the malcontents to leave the Reservation.

Among my scouts was one we called Dutchy, on account of his very German-like face. He had a keen sense of humor and we soon became fast friends. It was told of him that some ten or more years before, his father had killed a white man and had taken to the hills, where he defied all efforts at his capture, descending occasionally to harrass the occupants of some isolated Indian wikiup. The Agent, a portentous religious man, sent for Dutchy and so worked on his imagination by depicting the hell-fire and torment that would befall both Dutchy's own soul and that of his ancestor if his ancestor was permitted to continue in the paths of sin, that Dutchy was persuaded to undertake their mutual salvation.

The Agent provided him with a rifle, cartridges, rations for a week, and a sack in which to carry them. At the end of the week Dutchy returned. Going to the Agent with a smile of great satisfaction, he opened his sack and out of it rolled his ancestor's head at the Agent's feet.

I do not vouch for the story, but it was currently accepted as true among those who should know, Sieber and others. For my part, I found much of interest in my association with Dutchy. Our informal talks, for that matter all my informal talks with the Indians, were of fights with the Mexicans, or of hunting experiences. Fights with our own troops were tactfully tabu. Fighting, hunting, and gambling filled the Indian's life and were his sole topics of conversation.

One of Dutchy's stories is worth repeating; but to tell it I must tell the sequel first.

When I left the army it was to manage a mining and cattle property in the northwestern part of the state of Chihuahua, the heart of the Apache country, and my connection with the Indians did not entirely cease. Some time after taking charge of the property I had occasion to visit a newly discovered mine some forty miles to the northeast of my headquarters. On my way to the mine I passed through some brush-covered side hills and came upon what looked like the effect a cyclone might have on a small department store. For a mile or more the brush was strewn with long streamers of ginghams, muslins, calicos; the remains of rotting overalls, socks, shirts, and handkerchiefs. The ground was littered with cans of what had been canned fruit and vegetables, the cans of which had burst with the lapse of time and the desert heat. Cooking utensils and knives, forks, and spoons of a cheap class were rusting in the sun.

"What in the name of Heaven is all this?" I inquired of a Mexican who was with me.

"La derrota de Don Ramon" (the defeat of Don Ramon), he replied. Then he told me this story:

"Fifteen years ago there were no custom houses between the Rio Grande at El Paso and Fronteras in Sonora. Everybody that had any reason for getting things in the United States smuggled them. Don Ramon was a big man in the country and had lots of peons who needed American things. He used to go with a lot of pack mules to the American towns and bring them back loaded with anything he needed. The only thing he had to look out for was an attack by Indians. So he took with him a *conducta* (escort) of twenty men. For a long time he was lucky and the Indians did not catch him. Then one day they did.

"He was coming back with a full cargo of merchandise, when he was attacked by a large force of Indians. He and his men fought hard and killed a lot of Indians, but there were so many Indians that Don Ramon and his men were lucky to get away with their lives, but they lost the cargo, which the Indians wilfully destroyed. A few days later, with the help of some soldiers who had come from Sonora, they recovered the mules except two."

Then my subconscious mind demanded audience for Dutchy's story:

A band of the Indians were on one of their migrations from the mountains to the plains. Dutchy and two of his companions, the three of them about seventeen years of age, had dawdled behind the main body as boys always will. They saw the Mexican pack train approaching and in a spirit of pure bravado determined to see if they could "throw a scare" into the Mexicans who were guarding it. The brush was quite high and they had no fear that the Mexicans would follow them into it. Another thing in their favor was that the Mexicans had seen the dust raised by the horses of the Indian band not over two or three miles away and would naturally be apprehending an attack.

The only weapons Dutchy and his companions had were an old cap-and-ball six-shooter, an antiquated double-barreled shotgun, more dangerous to the shooter than to the shootee, and a bow and arrows. With these they lay in wait in a shallow gully fringed with heavy brush, near which they knew the train would pass.

At the psychological moment the old shotgun roared, Dutchy's blunderbuss of a revolver beat a tattoo, arrows flew from the bow-and-arrow boy, and the Indians sent up yells and war cries in as many different keys as they could devise.

"Make like seem heap Injin," as Dutchy described it.

The Mexicans waited not upon the order of their going but went at once, a trail of dust pointing their destination as the nearest Mexican town, some thirty miles away.

The warriors of the main band, hearing the firing, returned in haste to see what it was all about and found Dutchy and his pals in command of some sixty or seventy heavily loaded pack mules. Then the fun began.

An Indian on his pony would take hold of the end of a bolt of calico and away he would go over the hillside, the bolt unraveling behind him. The bushes properly festooned, he would return for another bolt. A pair of overalls were sufficient incitement to a tug of war. Two mounted Indians would each seize a leg, and as the tenacity of the Indians's legs exceeded that of the overalls, each Indian would "gain a leg" on the contest.

Socks and stockings in pairs were pulled over the top branches of bushes, looking like dozens of feet on a march to Heaven.

The men of the party put on as many shirts as each desired, the women selecting dress material for months to come and all the flour and other food they wanted. Everything else was destroyed as far as possible. A fat young mule was killed for a feast and the others were turned loose, as the Indians had no use for them.

The reader may take his choice of the two versions of what happened at *La derrota de Don Ramon.*

Dutchy also told me of an instance where an Indian was wounded in five places by the same bullet. He was crouching behind a small tree, firing at an enemy above him on a hillside. The bullet made flesh wounds in his arm above and below the elbow, in his leg above and below the knee, and in his foot. If you don't believe him, get behind a small tree and figure it out. I did.

FORT THOMAS IN 1882

AGENCY BUILDINGS, SAN CARLOS

GEN. GEORGE CROOK
COMMANDER

CAPT. EMMETT CRAWFORD,
THIRD CAVALRY

FIRST LIEUT. CHARLES B.
GATEWOOD, SIXTH CAVALRY

SECOND LIEUT. BRITTON
DAVIS, THIRD CAVALRY

AN APACHE BUNGALOW

LEFT—BENITO, CHIRICAHUA SUBCHIEF
RIGHT—DUTCHY

LOCO

Successor to Victorio in the post of war chief of the Warm Springs.

MANGUS

Son of Mangus Colorado, and as such, hereditary chief of the Warm Springs.

NACHITE

Son of Cochise, and as such hereditary chief of the Chiricahua.

AN APACHE SOUSA

Playing a primitive fiddle; with a collection of objects of tribal handicraft.

"DOUGHERTY WAGON," SLIGHTLY MODIFIED

This vehicle served as an officer's transport.

MY WAR STEED, BARNEY, READY FOR THE TRAIL

A Texan, I preferred a Texas saddle to the army saddle then used.

CHATTO—FIRST SERGT., CO. "B"
APACHE SCOUTS

KA-YA-TEN-NAE

His arrest at Turkey Creek risked a tragedy.

HEART OF THE CHIRICAHUA STRONGHOLD ON THE CREST OF THE SIERRA MADRE

THE SIERRA MADRE JUST NORTH OF THE RIO DE AROS, NEAR ITS JUNCTION WITH THE BAVISPE

The arrow points to the peak near which Crawford was killed.

SOME OF MY SCOUTS AT EL PASO

They wanted to be photographed but demanded that I first purchase for them clean clothes.

LEFT—MICKEY FREE. RIGHT—CHATTO

GERONIMO'S BAND ON THE WAY TO FLORIDA AFTER THEIR SURRENDER

Front row, third from left, Nachite; fourth, Geronimo; fifth, Geronimo's son, Chappo.

CROOK'S MEXICAN EXPEDITION, 1883

CROOK'S CONFERENCE WITH GERONIMO,
MARCH 25-26, 1886

TONTO WARRIORS STRIPPED FOR BATTLE

FORT APACHE IN 1882

Chapter VIII

The Kiowa chief's peace offering. The chiefs oppose certain of the General's orders. A turkey gobbler's good offices. Arrest of Ka-ya-ten-nae. An Apache dance. Arrest of Gar. We move down near Fort Apache. Snow in Arizona. Efforts at farming. Growing discontent fostered at San Carlos. Huera. Crawford leaves and Pierce takes his place.

THAT the Indian was sincere in a line of reasoning often incomprehensible to us could not be better illustrated than by the following incident: Shortly after his appointment in 1869 as Provisional Governor of Texas my father, the late Edmund J. Davis, went to Fort Worth, Texas, to negotiate a treaty of peace with the Comanche and Kiowa Indian tribes.

Chief Satanta of the Comanche and Subchief Big Tree of the Kiowa had been captured some two years previously and confined in the penitentiary at Huntsville, Texas. My father pardoned them and took them with him to restore them to their people who at that time occupied the country near Fort Worth.

The old head chief of the Kiowa was so grateful that he with a delegation of the principal Kiowa and Comanche chiefs came to my father to present him with the old Chief's most treasured possession—a beautiful robe made of six skins of the Lobo wolf, the great, gray wolf of the prairies, now practically if not entirely extinct. The robe was lined with red flannel and had an ornamented border.

But it was not the robe that the Chief prized. Wolf

skins at that time were plentiful and red flannel was to be had at any trader store. His several wives could do the work. The ornaments! His soul must have reached the acme of gratitude when he decided to part with them. They were human scalps set about a foot apart along two sides and one end of the robe. As the robe was eight feet by five the number of scalps may be computed by the curious.

The old Chief apologized for the incompleted end and told my father that if he had come to see them a little later he would have had it complete for him. Seeing an expression in my father's face that was certainly not disappointment the old Chief hastened to assure him that the scalps were all Mexican and Indian—"no squaw, no Blancos" (no women, no Whites).

My father was diplomatic. In turn he assured the old Chief that he was well aware that scalps were evidence of the prowess of a warrior, and that he, my father, could not think of depriving so great a warrior of this proof of his greatness. If the Chief would remove the scalps and retain them my father would be pleased to receive the robe in token of the eternal peace that was now to exist between the Kiowas, Comanches, and all the people who inhabited the state of Texas. The robe would be the token that all might now sleep secure.

The old Chief was delighted at the suggestion and so it was arranged to the satisfaction of all the parties concerned.

Conditions at Turkey Creek were not entirely satisfactory. None of the Indians were making anything more than a bluff at farming; a few were half-heartedly clearing some of the brush from little patches of ground here and there in the river bottom near Fort Apache.

Most of them contented themselves with loafing and gambling, or trading some of their ponies for things they wanted from the White Mountain. A band of Navaho came down and took more of the ponies away in exchange for Navaho blankets.

My principal concern was Ka-ya-ten-nae. He and his band were almost openly antagonistic. Secret service scouts reported that he regretted having come to the Reservation and was telling the other Indians that they were fools for having done so. Also, he was advising resistance to the General's orders against making tizwin and brutally beating their wives. Little attention was paid to these orders and I finally called the chiefs to my tent and told them that further offenses along these lines would land the offender in the Apache calaboose.

The chiefs were nearly unanimous in their protests against the orders. They said that they had made no such agreement with the General when they had their talk with him in Mexico; that their agreement was to keep the peace with whites, Mexicans, and Indians. This they had done and were doing. No mention had been made of their family affairs, and they were free to conduct them as they saw fit. As for making tizwin, the white officers and soldiers and all the white men and Mexicans drank some sort of liquor to make them feel good. Why should the same thing be forbidden the Indians? They had always made tizwin and it had done them no harm. They did not want any of their people put in jail for making it.

Chihuahua, especially, was determined in his opposition to the order prohibiting tizwin, for Chihuahua loved his toddy. Ka-ya-ten-nae was silent and surly. The meeting broke up with no agreement by the chiefs to accept the General's orders and no concessions on my part in the matter of enforcement. Later Ka-ya-ten-nae was reported to be advising resistance to any attempt at arrest.

While things were in this condition I received a message from West at San Carlos that he was coming up for a turkey dinner and a short visit. On the morning of the day he was to arrive I rode up the creek to get a turkey. A mile or two above my camp a trail led up from the creek bottom to the mesa above. Finding no turkeys in the creek bottom I decided to try the mesa. Half way up the trail I heard a turkey gobble in the creek bottom some little distance above where I had left it. For a moment I was undecided whether to go on up to the mesa or return and go after the chap that had challenged me from the creek.

Finally deciding on the latter, I rode back down the trail, went up the creek, and got a turkey; but it has been my life-long hope that I did not get the gobbler that called me back.

West arrived, we had our turkey dinner, and, after the usual smoke and talk, turned in. Hardly had we put out the candle when a pebble hit the top of my tent and rolled down its side—the signal from a secret service scout. Crawling under the rear wall of my tent and going some twenty steps north, as we had arranged for such meetings, I found Mickey and one of the scouts, the woman, behind a giant pine. The first thing she asked was why I had that morning turned back on the trail out of the creek bed. I told her.

"That was the good spirit of one of your ancestors in that gobbler," she said, then went on to explain what she had come about.

When I started up the trail from the creek bed Ka-ya-ten-nae and his band were having a tizwin drunk on the mesa just where the trail came out on it. Seeing me coming up the trail with my rifle, they thought that I had heard of the drunk and was coming to arrest them and put them in jail at Fort Apache. Getting their guns, they lay down near the top of the trail and waited for me. Had I shown my head above the edge of the bluff it would have received more lead than it could well have accommodated.

The band had decided to have the drunk in defiance of orders, make no attempt at concealment, and if I came with scouts or alone to arrest them, kill me and anyone with me, stampede as many more of the Indians as possible, and make a break for Mexico. Only my turning back down the trail that morning had spoiled the plan, and the band could not understand why I had turned back. A similar plan bore fruit the following spring.

To think that I had eaten that turkey! My only consolation was in the certainty that at least I had not eaten the kindly spirit of my ancestor.

Returning to my tent, I told West that I was going to arrest Ka-ya-ten-nae at sunrise the next morning and send him to San Carlos. It was going to be a ticklish business. We were not yet three years away from the Cibicu massacre of August 30, 1881, where Captain Hentig and several of his men were killed in the attempt to arrest the medicine man, Noch-a-del-klinne; an attempt that resulted in the mutiny of a part of Lieutenant Cruse's scouts.

A month later, September 30, the agency chief of police, Sterling, was killed at the Camp Goodwin sub-agency in attempting to arrest an Indian there. The killing of Sterling was followed by an outbreak, some three hundred of the Indians under Juh and Geronimo leaving the Reservation and escaping to Mexico. In fact our army history is replete with similar incidents growing out of attempts to arrest individual Indians for crimes committed, or for other reasons arising in the conduct of Indian affairs.

So here was a condition that could no longer be ignored; a condition that must be met as those other conditions were met, without opportunity to forestall the consequences that might arise. The one rotten apple in the pile would soon affect others. Ka-ya-ten-nae was only waiting until he could corrupt a sufficiently large following, which as yet he had been unable to do on account of the opposition of several of the chiefs. Those opposing him were Chato, Benito, Loco, Mangus, and Zele. Nachite and Geronimo held aloof. Old Nana counseled patience but got little attention.

What would happen when I attempted the arrest no one could possibly foresee. Ka-ya-ten-nae had an immediate following of thirty-two of the most reckless of the young braves. That they would stick by him I felt sure, but what the other Indians would think of his arrest I could not predict. It would be a stunning surprise to them and their reaction to it might be anything; he was looked upon as the coming war chief of the combined Chiricahua and Warm Springs bands had they remained in Mexico. If the reaction of the great majority was for peace at any price, I could get away with the arrest. If, however, it was for war, I was determined that the Indians should not be the only ones to make a killing.

I asked West to ride in at once to Fort Apache, seventeen miles away, explain the situation to the commanding officer, and request that the four troops of cavalry there, about 140 men, be sent out to reach my tent just at sunrise. This was the moment I had decided as best to attempt the arrest as it was about the time I usually met the chiefs for important talks.

At the first signs of day I sent some of the scouts to call the chiefs to my tent; some of them lived two or three miles away. Ka-ya-ten-nae, however, as I have said, had his personal camp on the ridge just above mine.

The sun was not quite up when West came to tell me that the four troops of cavalry were just behind him. I sent him back to stop them some two hundred yards back of my tent, where the chiefs and principal men were now assembling. The large hospital tent in which we held our talks faced away from the troops. Ka-ya-ten-nae, although camped nearer to me than any of the others, had not come. Usually a number of women and children would be seen at this time of the day in the pine timber around my camp. Now not one was in sight. In the tent were about twenty of the chiefs and principal men. Outside it were two or three times as many. All had their arms with them, partly concealed under their blankets. Never before had they come for a talk armed. Evidently the coming of the soldiers had been noted and the Indian telegraph put at work shortly after the troops had left the post.

The chiefs asked why I had sent for them. I told them I would let them know as soon as Ka-ya-ten-nae arrived, and sent for him again. Presently he came down the hill with his followers behind him. They stopped under a pine tree about a hundred yards in front of the tent, where Ka-ya-ten-nae spoke a few words to them then came on alone. On his cartridge belt full of cartridges, hung his revolver; he had doubtless left his rifle with his men.

Evidently he knew that he was the cause of the commotion, for he strode up to within three feet of me before he stopped and demanded angrily why I had sent for him. I told him that he had never been satisfied since he had come upon the Reservation and was causing trouble and dissatisfaction among the other Indians; that Captain Crawford had warned him before he came to Turkey Creek, but the warning had done no good and I was going to send him back to San Carlos for Captain Crawford to deal with.

He demanded to know who was accusing him of making trouble. I told him he would learn that and what he was accused of when he arrived at San Carlos, not before. That those were my orders from Crawford in case he caused more trouble, and my orders would be carried out.

For a moment he stood staring me in the face, then, without a word, wheeled in his tracks and started for his men. As soon as they saw his move they spread out, leveled their guns, and started toward the tent to meet him, breech locks clicking as they came on.

As Ka-ya-ten-nae started for his men, two scouts who had been standing behind me, Dutchy and a scout we called Charley, started after him with their rifles cocked and ready. Afterward, I asked them what they proposed to do and they told me they had determined to get Ka-ya-ten-nae at least, if he and his men started anything; then they were going to fight it out with the band.

How is that for the treachery of Indians? Certain death for them!

The situation for the half-minute or so that it took

Ka-ya-ten-nae and his men to cover the distance between that pine tree and my tent was not one I can recommend for jumpy nerves. Around me, in the door of the tent, were a score of chiefs and principal men; outside the tent were fifty or sixty more, with no attempts now being made to conceal weapons. Some two hundred yards back of me were the four troops of cavalry, dismounted in line and ready for anything that might turn up. They could not see what was going on at the tent, a very large one and between them and Ka-ya-ten-nae's band. If a rumpus started they could only be expected to use reasonable discretion when they took a hand in it. To me it seemed a three-cornered bet as to who would get me—Ka-ya-ten-nae's band, the Indians around me, or the troops in the rear.

Halfway to the pine tree Ka-ya-ten-nae met his men, turned and came with them. Ten feet from me he halted them but came on himself until he was at arm's length. Trembling with rage so that he could hardly speak, he demanded that I should point out to him which of his men had accused him.

He had weakened and there would be no fight!

I repeated what I had told him before, that he would know who accused him when he got to San Carlos.

Reaching out, I unbuckled his cartridge belt with the revolver and threw it over my arm, telling him he was under arrest and would be sent to San Carlos at once with some of the scouts. My action in taking the belt and revolver from him had a queer result—he seemed suddenly to wilt, his bravado falling from him like a discarded cloak.

Benito immediately stepped forward from the Indians around us and offered himself and Charley as hostages for Ka-ya-ten-nae's safe delivery at San Carlos if I would return his arms and permit him to go as a warrior. It was as if the sun had suddenly broken through the clouds and I felt almost like dancing a jig from sheer relief as I turned the belt and pistol over to Benito and went to tell the officer in command of the troops, Captain Allan Smith of the Fourth Cavalry, that there would be no trouble and the troops could return to the post.

Half an hour later Ka-ya-ten-nae was on his way to San Carlos, "armed as a warrior should be," with his two sureties. He was tried and convicted by an Indian jury and sentenced by Crawford to five years' imprisonment in Alcatraz prison, California. After serving about eighteen months of his sentence he was pardoned by General Crook and assisted the General greatly in his efforts to secure the surrender of the few hostiles still in Mexico in the spring of 1886.

Many years after this incident I met, at a West Point dinner, one of the officers who had been with Captain Smith's command at Turkey Creek, and he paid me this compliment:

"Davis, I thought you were the damnedest fool I had ever known, in the army or out."

So you see I proved the truth of the old adage, "A fool for luck!" But I have often wondered what that quiet, sunlit little glen in the pines would have looked like ten seconds after some nervous chap, white or red, had let the hammer of his rifle slip.

With the arrest of Ka-ya-ten-nae, peace reigned in camp and the first snappy day of fall was the signal for a "heap big dance," to celebrate properly the annual trek to the lowlands beyond the reach of snow; a custom as old, almost, as the tribe itself; for such had been their custom in Mexico and the Southwest for centuries before the coming of the white man.

In fact, there were to be two dances—a score of young men were first to exhibit their grace, this to be followed by a dance in which all who desired could take part. I do not know the significance of the young-man dance, if it had any significance; but of one thing I fully approved—they were to take a sweat bath! When an Apache had worn a shirt so long that he thought a new one was coming to him, he simply put the new one on over the old one. If he had no woman to launder for him, and sometimes even if he had, he left the fate of the old shirt to Nature.

The preparation for the bath was simple but effective. A number of long, pliable twigs were set in the ground around a circle twelve or fifteen feet in diameter. The tops of the twigs were then bent to the middle, tied, and the whole framework covered with cloths. On one side a low opening was left for a door, which was closed by a dropped piece of blanket.

While two women were engaged in building the steam room about ten feet from the bank of the creek, which its door faced, another woman had built a fire nearby and was rolling into it three or four rocks the size of a person's head. A camp kettle of water had been brought to a boil and placed in the hut, and all was now ready.

The young braves arrived stripped to their breechcloths and entered the hut. Seated in a circle about the camp kettle, they raised their voices in mournful song. From time to time one of the women would roll a red-hot rock to the door, where a brave would sieze it with sticks and deposit it in the kettle. The steam arising from the combination gave a very good imitation of a Turkish bath. When the young men considered that they had been sufficiently purified they rushed out and plunged into the icy waters of the creek.

Only the pen of a Dante or the brush of a Michael Angelo could make anything interesting out of an Apache dance. A lame description of it would only bore the reader. But the setting was one of wonderful beauty. The grass-covered glade on the mountain top; the giant pines standing like a mass of well-ordered spectators, and throwing back from their glistening leaves a red reflection of the great bonfire from which the sparks rose straight up to the stars above; beyond the circle of the fire, black night stretching back through the forest that seemed without end; the almost nude figures of the Indian dancers, fantastically painted, bobbing up and down to the rhythm of the Indian drums and cheered to a frenzy of movement by the yells of over half a thousand spectators—was this reality, and civilization only a dream? I was reliving a previous existence.

For miles around notice of the dance had gone and other tribes had been invited. Following the dance of the young men the feasting began, to the accompaniment of the drums and a general dance for all. For this latter, a long line was formed, the young men and the young women, arm in arm, alternating in the line. The dance itself was a monotonous forward and back movement to the crooning of a song that alternately rose almost to a shout to fall almost to a whisper.

Gatewood and Roach had come out from the post on a combination visit of pleasure and business. The business had to do with the escape from the jail at Fort Apache of an Indian known as Gar. Gar had been put in durance vile for some offense or other, I don't remember what, but had escaped some weeks before and Gatewood had been unable to recapture him. Thinking that Gar might not be able to resist the lure of the dance and feast, especially as he was related to some of the Chiricahua, Gatewood hoped he might put in an appearance.

About midnight Gatewood's hopes were realized. Two of my scouts came to me with the information that Gar was in the line of dancers, near the end, in the obscurity of the shadows cast by the pines. Executing a flank movement through the pine timber with my two scouts, followed by an attack from the rear, all in accord with proper military tactics, a bloodless victory was achieved and the enemy captured. And he was certainly a scared Indian. He spoke some English and began at once to beg me for his life, although I had not the least idea of taking it.

"Done shoot me, Lieutenant! Done shoot me!" he begged. "I be good Injin. I do what you say, you done shoot me."

My scouts took him back to Fort Apache with Gatewood, where he served the rest of his term in jail and became "good Injin" thereafter so far as I know.

With the first snow we moved camp down to the White River bottom near Fort Apache, my own camp being pitched about three miles above the post, while the Indians camped in the foothills or above me on the river. Here we remained for the three months of winter with no incident of importance other than a foolhardy trip to San Carlos in a blizzard for the sake of a baseball game.

If you have never tackled a blizzard in the mountains with four feet of snow under foot and no protection other than the ordinary army clothing worn in Arizona, you have a thrill ahead of you—that is providing you like those thrills that make you guess whether or not your obituary will appear in the home papers next spring.

In the fall our San Carlos baseball team, of which I was first baseman, had beaten the team from Globe by a score of thirty-one to thirty and relieved them of much of their spare cash. They demanded a return match to be played at Globe. I may as well admit here that they won twelve to nine and got back their cash with compound interest. I can say truthfully that I did not lose that game for I know who did. I will not mention his name as he may still be alive and might sue me for libel. But I will say this much—our shortstop was Lieutenant Dugan. Now a shortstop who puts his knees together and leaves his feet a foot apart doesn't throw much of a scare into the opposition, and more than his share of batted balls are likely to come his way.

Crawford had sent a packer and pack mule to accompany me to San Carlos. When we left Fort Apache at noon it was snowing, but melting at that altitude. Ten miles up the mountain side the snow was two feet deep and falling fast. Five miles farther on we camped for the night. All night it snowed and in the morning it was three to four feet on a level, with drifts twice as deep and a blizzard blowing. The packer Crawford had sent was a cripple, one leg being a little shorter than the other. By midafternoon he was nearly all in and I was but little better off. We had to walk to keep from freezing. Crossing Black River, our pack mule had slipped and fallen in the stream. His struggles to regain his feet only served to soak our bedding, which by now was a frozen mass. To stop and camp was worse than to struggle on.

Fortunately, my saddle mule was a very intelligent and powerful ex-citizen of Missouri. He had the mule instinct of knowing where he was bound and a desire to be on his way. Neither the packer nor I could see the road through the blinding storm; to lose it might have dropped us over the edge of a cañon with disastrous results. I lengthened the reins of my mule's bridle with a couple of pieces of string and drove him ahead of us to break trail, trusting to his keeping the path through the wilderness of pine timber.

Three hours of this, then night came on and we had decided to take our chances in the frozen blankets when the road suddenly dipped down into a cañon we recognized as the lead down to the Gila bottom. Two hours later we were below the snow and before a bonfire, which we had just strength enough left to build and drop down beside. A week later I again traveled this trail in bright sunshine, after it had been broken by the passage of a couple of pack trains on their way from Fort Thomas to Fort Apache, and wondered at the bad day it had given me.

At Turkey Creek my quarters had been an ordinary eight-foot A tent with a dirt floor. At Fort Apache the quartermaster fitted me up luxuriously with a twelve-foot walltent, floored, and the sides boarded up to the eaves of the roof. A frame in the front, in which was fitted a canvas door, completed it. Talks with the chiefs were now held in this tent, the hospital tent serving only as a storeroom and place to issue rations.

This issue of rations took the better part of a day each week and was no sinecure. About 150 different sets of rations had to be ladled out by cupfuls according to the number of people in a family—coffee, sugar, beans, and flour, with small portions of salt, pepper, and baking powder. The meat ration was now issued at the Apache slaughter pen. The issue of rations had been my job since we reached Turkey Creek as neither Bowman nor Mickey, both illiterate, were equal to it.

A curious sight at these ration issues would often be a lone Indian man, seated at a distance from the women and children gathered to receive their rations, his head covered with his blanket or a piece of cotton sheeting, waiting patiently until some particular woman should leave the gathering. The woman in question was his mother-in-law. His wife, for some reason had been unable to come for their rations and had sent him. Indian etiquette required that a mother-in-law should never see the face of her son-in-law, and the burden of compliance was his.

With the coming of spring the Indians set about making some effort at farming; but the actual work done by most of them was delegated to the women. A round-up of tools and implements showed that a number were missing. They had been sold or gambled off to the Cibucu or White Mountain Indians, who were more interested in farming than were the majority of the recent hostiles. Several of the wagons were in need of repair, having been smashed in wild rides over trackless mountain sides.

Geronimo's efforts at self-support were typical of the efforts of many. He came to me one day with the request that I visit his "farm." I could not go at the moment but went the following morning. He had shown me a small blister on the palm of one of his hands, of which he was very proud. When I arrived at the section of river bottom that had been allotted to him and his band he was sitting on a rail in the shade of a tree with one of his wives fanning him. The other two were hoeing a quarter-acre patch of partially cleared ground, in which a few sickly looking sprouts of corn were struggling for life.

The Indians were not entirely to blame. They were being forced into a mode of life foreign to their nature, in a location as little adapted to agriculture as the Adirondack Mountains of New York. Anywhere out of the river bottoms only precarious dry farming was possible. Even in the river bottoms irrigating ditches were necessary, as there was not moisture sufficient to grow crops profitably without irrigation. The most suitable sections of land for farming purposes in the vicinity of Fort Apache had been assigned to the White Mountain, Cibucu, and Coyotero several years before. The newcomers had to take what was left.

Bowman was doing all he could as farm instructor, and I was planning a dam and irrigation ditch in the White River bottom when the storm broke and wrote Finis to our efforts to teach a Chiricahua Indian that there were other uses for the handle of a hoe than to settle conjugal differences of opinion.

Looking back on the events of those three months of March, April, and May, 1885, incidents which then seemed inconsequential loom now as portents pointing to the disaster that was to follow. The stage was being set for a tragedy that demanded the lives of two of the finest of our officers of the old army, eight of our regular soldiers, four score American settlers (seventy-three actually recorded), twelve reservation Indians, and an unknown number of Mexicans; a tragedy that cast the shadow of unmerited censure over the closing days of the brilliant career of a general of the army, bestowing honor where honor was not due; and whose only high light in the dull horror of massacre and fruitless pursuit was one example of personal courage as fine as any army can boast.

All was not well at San Carlos. Agent Willcox, who had been content to leave in the hands of the military all police control of the Indians, was relieved in December, 1884, by Agent Ford, a man with little knowledge of Indians in general, and especially ignorant of anything concerning an Apache. But he was determined to assert his authority as Agent, and friction had at once begun between him and Crawford. The Indian Bureau, now that there had been no difficulties with the Indians for nearly two years, assumed that the time had come for the political gang to resume their grafting. It would never do to let these Indians become self-supporting, as political patronage would suffer and a great howl would go up from the contractors who were supplying the Indians with the necessities of life.

The position of agency chief of police, which had been abandoned when we took over the control of the Reservation after the killing of Colvig, was resurrected and a new chief appointed by the Agent. Jealous of the efforts Crawford was making to get the Indians into systematic farming by taking out irrigating ditches and properly preparing their farms, an agency head farmer was appointed. These two men immediately set themselves up in opposition to Crawford and his assistants. The chief of police shielded men Crawford wanted to arrest; and the farmer, backed by the Agent, stopped work Dugan had begun on ditches and forbade other work.

The Apache is no fool. He quickly saw the condition

of affairs and at once took advantage of it. Denied by the military he appealed to the Agent, or *vice versa.* There is no need to point out how quickly such a situation will destroy control even of a civilized community; with the restless element among these Indians it was quicker, and more deadly in the aftermath. In this division of authority and consequent friction at San Carlos I find the fundamental cause of the outbreak of May 17. The seed of divided authority sprouts and bears its natural fruit—defiance of all authority.

Defiance of authority at San Carlos soon spread to my camp at Fort Apache. Tizwin drinking reappeared. Reports of brutal beating of women came to me, but the women refused to complain. Finally, however, a young woman came to me with her left arm broken in two places, her hair matted with blood, and her shoulders a mass of welts and bruises. Her husband, a man of middle age, had disciplined her with a stick of wood. I arrested him and locked him up in the jail at Fort Apache. Several of the chiefs came to me with a demand for his release; a demand I refused pending his serving a two weeks' sentence. By that time the post surgeon had repaired the bride and made her ready to endure a few more love pats when her lord and master felt so inclined.

Tired of ineffectual admonition and threats in the matter of tizwin making, I arrested an Indian responsible for a drunk and lodged him also in the calaboose at Fort Apache. That afternoon Chihuahua and Mangus came to my tent with a vigorous protest. I was not surprised to hear from Chihuahua on this subject as he was a leading protestant on all matters of discipline. But Mangus had theretofore been one of the most tractable of the Indians, he and old Loco frequently backing me up in controversies. That night I learned from one of my secret service scouts the cause of this attitude on the part of Mangus.

When the General had returned with the hostiles from Mexico he had brought with him a number of Mexican women who had been captives among them. These women had been restored to their families in Mexico. In turn, some Indian women who had been captives among the Mexicans were restored to their people at San Carlos. Among these was a woman about forty years of age known as Huera, one of Mangus' wives. She spoke Spanish well and we tried to use her as an interpreter; but for some reason she was very bitter against us, refusing to have anything to do with helping us and never came near me even to draw rations, always sending one of the younger women. She, I found out, was a skilful tizwin maker and her wares were in great demand. In this lay Mangus' interest, and her determined fight to continue her trade was an important factor in stiffening the resistance of the Indians to my prohibition efforts. Her years among the Mexicans and her knowledge of Spanish gave her considerable influence among the turbulent set.

Another malcontent, who it later developed was backing her up and preaching the gospel of resistance, was an Indian known as Nadiskay. This Indian was a Coyotero married to a Chiricahua. During my stay on the Mexican border while waiting for Geronimo to come in, Crawford had sent him to the calaboose at Fort Thomas for some offense or other. When we removed to Turkey Creek he was released and went with us. His punishment had served only to embitter him and he became at once a thorn in my side. I heard reports of his talks but could never fix anything positive on him as he was very guarded in what he said and careful in selecting his listeners. All I could get was second- or third-hand hearsay.

Another source of contention with the Chiricahua and Warm Springs was the restoration of the right of a husband to cut off the nose of an unfaithful wife. This practice had been broken up by the General while he was in command of the Department in 1873. The returned hostiles contended that as they were never a party to such a regulation they were not to be bound by it. Among the Indians of the Reservation there were about a score of women so disfigured, and the General was emphatic that the practice should stop.

Affairs went from bad to worse at San Carlos. Twice the General had agreed with the Interior Department for police control of the Reservation, and twice the Indian Bureau at Washington had immediately set about nullifying the agreement. Their first efforts had failed; now they were succeeding. The territorial newspapers were continuing their attacks on Crook and Crawford, backed by whatever assistance and encouragement the Agent and his satellites could give them. Attacks on Crawford and friction between him and the Agent became so bitter that Crawford was forced to call for a Board of Inquiry. The board sustained him in every particular; but Crawford, embittered, asked to be relieved to rejoin his troop in Texas. The General, unable to cope with the political gang in Washington, acceded to his wish and Captain Pierce of the First Infantry was appointed to succeed him.

The change from Crawford to Pierce at this critical time was fatal. I cannot call it an error on the General's part, for he could not possibly have foreseen what was to follow.

I do not wish it to be inferred that the trouble at San Carlos was the sole cause of the outbreak of May 17. It was only a contributing cause, but it was an important one; and Crawford's removal had a fatal result in the effectiveness of the outbreak.

The fundamental cause was the dissatisfaction of three small factions among the Indians, led by Chihuahua, Mangus, and Geronimo. These factions combined did not number more than a dozen or fifteen men, the rest of the Indians accepting the situation in good faith and honestly desiring to keep the peace. Chihuahua's discontent, like that of Mangus, was confined to the regulations forbidding the drinking of tizwin and ill treatment of women. Geronimo's dissatisfaction was deeper seated and far more serious.

This Indian was a thoroughly vicious, intractable, and treacherous man. His only redeeming traits were courage and determination. His word, no matter how earnestly pledged, was worthless. His history past and to follow was a series of broken pledges and incitements to outbreaks. He and Juh had caused the outbreak of September, 1881; he was the leader of the band that forced Loco and his people to leave the Reservation in April, 1882. Notwithstanding his promise to the General in Mexico that he would come to the Reservation as soon as he could gather his people, he did not come in until a year later, the last of the bands to reach San Carlos. In March, 1886, at Cañon de los Embudos in Sonora, he surrendered to General Crook with many pledges of future good behavior. That night he and Nachite got drunk and with eighteen of their followers, accompanied by thirteen women and two children, he again took the warpath.

When on his return from Mexico in the spring of 1884 he was told that he would have to give up the cattle he had stolen from the Mexicans, he was so enraged that he would have left the Reservation then and there had he been able to count upon a sufficiently large following to make the attempt successful. Failing this, he sulked in his camp. The arrest and imprisonment of Ka-ya-ten-nae made him cautious and he smothered his resentment until fortune favored him with the opportunity for which he wished and waited.

I am reliably informed that to his dying day he regretted the agreement he made with Gatewood, under which he surrendered to Miles in September, 1886. The last years of his life were spent at Fort Sill, Indian Territory, where he is quoted as having said a short time before his death that he had much better have remained in the mountains of Mexico and fought it out to the end.

Chihuahua was egged on by Mangus, whose personal following was small. I do not believe that either of them wished or expected the trouble to go so far as an outbreak. Mangus, in the interest of Huera, wanted the right to make tizwin and Chihuahua wanted the right to drink it. Geronimo, thoroughly dissatisfied, took advantage of the situation.

Chapter IX

The outbreak. I take the field. Brush with Chihuahua's band. They attack Hatfield's camp. I meet Crawford. We enter Mexico. Sieber and the bearskins. A mescal distillery. Sieber has his joke. An ex-Confederate soldier. Valuable paintings.

A LITTLE before sunrise on the morning of May 15, I came out of my tent to find all the chiefs and subchiefs with about thirty of their followers waiting for me. They said they had come for a talk. Not a woman or child was in sight, a sure sign of something serious in the air. Near my tent was a small knoll from the top of which any movement of troops from Fort Apache could be seen as soon as they left the post. Two or three Indians had climbed the knoll and were watching the post. These men and a number of others were armed with rifles. The chiefs and subchiefs were unarmed except for a revolver here and there and the inevitable bowie knife. The scouts were standing around in groups of four or five here and there, all under arms.

The chiefs and subchiefs, with the exception of Chato, who remained outside with the scouts, entered the tent and squatted in a half circle on the floor in front of me. Loco began a slow and halting harangue. Chihuahua impatiently interrupted him and springing to his feet, said:

"What I have to say can be said in a few words. Then Loco can take all the rest of the day to talk if he wishes to do so."

Chihuahua then went on to repeat his previous argu-

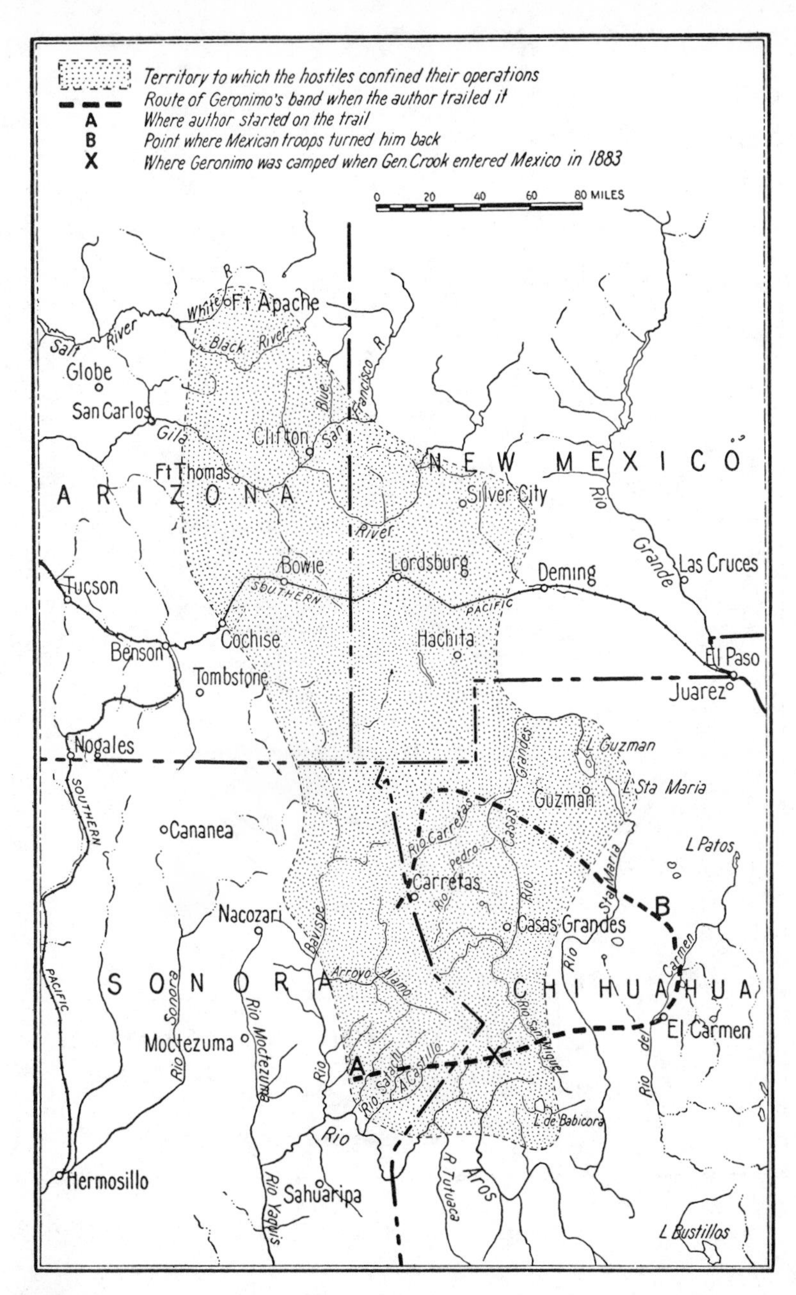

FIELD OF OPERATIONS IN GERONIMO CAMPAIGN

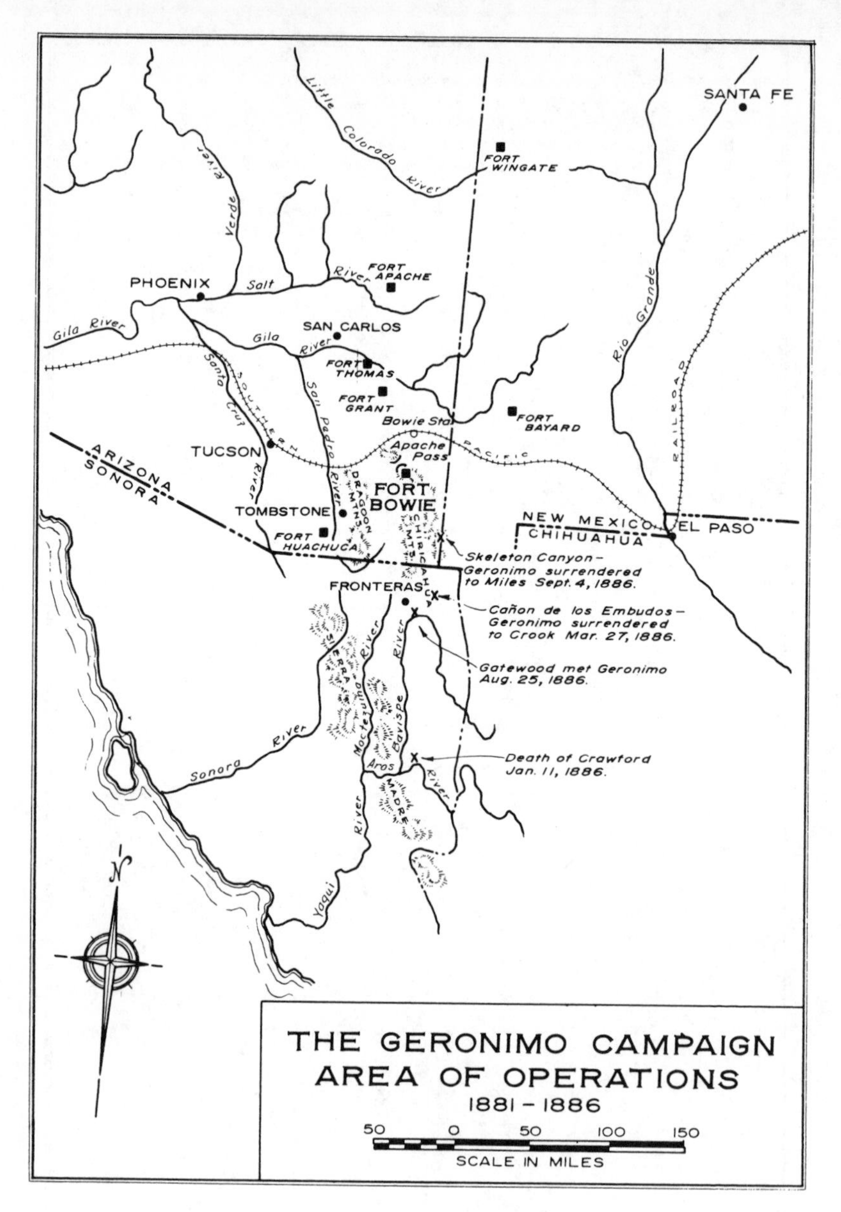

Courtesy of the National Park Service

ments on the subjects of wife beating and tizwin drinking. They had agreed on a peace with Americans, Mexicans, and other Indian tribes; nothing had been said about their conduct among themselves; they were not children to be taught how to live with their women and what they should eat or drink. All their lives they had eaten and drunk what seemed good to them. The white men drank wine and whiskey, even the officers and soldiers of the posts. The treatment of their wives was their own business. They were not ill treated when they behaved. When a woman would not behave the husband had a right to punish her. They had complied with all they had promised to do when they had their talk with the General in Mexico; had kept the peace and harmed no one. Now they were being punished for things they had a right to do so long as they did no harm to others.

I reminded them of the General's reasons for prohibiting tizwin—that an Indian drunk did not know what he was doing and might kill another of a different tribe, causing war between tribes of the Reservation or even an outbreak. I mentioned a case where a drunken Chiricahua not more than a month before had attempted to kill his wife, stabbing her in the shoulder before others interfered and saved her. The Indians had hushed this up, doctoring the woman themselves, and thought I did not know of it.

I began something in regard to the wife beating. Old Nana got up, said an angry sentence or two to Mickey Free, and stalked out of the tent. I asked Mickey what Nana had said and Mickey tried to dodge the answer. When I insisted, he translated:

"Tell the *Nantan Enchau* (stout chief; Crawford and Gatewood were both rawboned) that he can't advise me how to treat my women. He is only a boy. I killed *men* before he was born."

That was a solar plexus blow to my dignity, and from the grunts of approval I saw that it was futile to pursue the matter further; the motion to establish a League for Woman's Rights had been unanimously voted down. Chihuahua resumed the argument, if one-sided statement of a bill of rights may be called an argument.

"We all drank tizwin last night," he continued, "all of us in the tent and outside, except the scouts; and many more. What are you going to do about it? Are you going to put us all in jail? You have no jail big enough even if you could put us all in jail."

Since the replacement of Crawford by Pierce the Indians, especially Geronimo, had frequently asked me if *Nantan Lupan* (Gray Wolf chief, the General) was still in charge of them. Crawford, Elliott, Agent Willcox, and Colonel Beaumont, all known to them, had gone; Pierce, Ford, and their assistants were strangers. Naturally the Indians inferred that *Nantan Lupan,* the man they most feared, but upon whom they most relied for protection, had also left them. Like children, one answer to their question did not suffice; it must be answered again and again to reassure them. And at that I am sure that some of them did not believe me, for one of the arguments Geronimo used to induce them to leave the Reservation was that Crook also had gone away.

I told Chihuahua that what to do about the drink was too serious for me to decide. I was simply carrying out the General's orders, which he had given for their own good. I would wire him at once and request instructions, which I would make known to them as soon as I received them.

Benito and Zele started to say something but were interrupted by an angry protest from Chihuahua, who of all those present was the only one evidently under the influence of liquor; he was palpably drunk and in an ugly humor. With the exception of Loco's feeble effort, neither Geronimo nor any of the others had taken part in the discussion.

Wiring the General was not as simple a matter as it might seem. Captain Pierce, having relieved Crawford, was my commander. Under military requirements my telegrams were sent through him, to be forwarded with such approval, disapproval, or comments as he might see fit to make. Telegrams from San Carlos were sent to Willcox Station of the Pacific Railroad to be relayed over the railroad's lines to Maricopa, where they were again relayed over the military line to Whipple Barracks near Prescott.

Leaks over this line were frequent. The territorial newspapers were eager to get hold of anything that looked like a sensation, especially if it promised something detrimental to the General. We had to be very guarded in what we wired and, under the General's orders, confine ourselves to a bare statement of facts. He was so conversant with every phase of the matter in hand that no suggestions or comments were necessary for his immediate appreciation of any situation that might arise. By mail I reported weekly; oftener if the occasion warranted.

Due to the unfortunate loss of most of my records I cannot give verbatim the wording of my telegram, but it was essentially as follows:

"Captain F. E. Pierce, Commanding, San Carlos, Arizona.

"This morning all the chiefs and principal men came to my tent and said they wanted to talk. Chihuahua as spokesman said that when they agreed to come to the Reservation nothing had been said about their treatment of their women or drinking tizwin, for which they were now being punished. That the night before all of them except the scouts had been drinking tizwin. What was I going to do about it? Was I going to lock them all up?

"I told them that the matter was too serious for me to decide. That I would telegraph the fact to the General and do whatever he ordered me to do."

Captain Pierce had been at San Carlos only a little more than two months, knew almost nothing of the Apache of this Reservation, and had never so much as seen a Chiricahua. He was relying on Al Sieber for advice in every situation that arose. On receiving my telegram he took it to Sieber. Sieber had been up the night before gambling and drinking and was asleep. Pierce woke him up and showed him the telegram. Sieber read it and returned it with the remark:

"It's nothing but a tizwin drunk. Don't pay any attention to it. Davis will handle it," and went to sleep again. Pierce thereupon returned to his office and pigeonholed the telegram.

When on my return four months later from the campaign in Mexico I reported to the General at Bowie, he told me that the newspapers had made much of a telegram I was supposed to have sent him; but as he had never received such a message he felt sure none had been sent. I told him what I had sent and on his order got the telegram from Pierce at San Carlos and sent it to him.

A year later, after I had resigned from the army, I called on the General in Chicago, where he was then in command of the Division. He referred to this telegram and said that had he received it the outbreak would very probably never have occurred; and if it had occurred the Indians would never have reached Mexico but would have been taught a lesson they would never have forgotten. In which I fully agree.

Had Crawford been at San Carlos he would have realized the critical situation and have forwarded the telegram, saving the lives of many unfortunates as well as his own. But fate decreed otherwise.

Friday, Saturday, and most of Sunday passed without a reply from the General. I inferred, of course, that he was making preparations to deal with the situation and that I would have his orders when he was ready. I could not conceive that Pierce had not forwarded my wire, as it was so plainly intended for the General; and to have wired the General again would have been an impertinence unless I had something to say of a change in conditions. But there was none. I saw some of the malcontents every day and had frequent reports from the scouts. The Indians seemed to be waiting, as I was, for word from the General.

Sunday afternoon there was a baseball game between two post nines that I was asked to umpire while I was waiting at the post for a reply to my telegram. In the midst of the game, about four o'clock in the afternoon, Mickey and Chato came to me with the report that a number of Indians, they did not know how many, had left their camps and were on their way to Mexico.

I attempted at once to send a telegram to Captain Pierce advising him of this, but the operator found that the wires had been cut. It was not until the next day near noon that the break was found. The Indians had cut the line in the fork of a tree and tied it with a buckskin thong. My telegram then went through and was forwarded to the General, but too late for him to put into effect any plans he might have had in mind.

Colonel Wade, in command of the troops at Fort Apache, immediately ordered them to prepare to take the field, but it was dark before they were ready. I returned to my tent to prepare my scouts to accompany them. The scouts were drawn up in front of my tent to have additional cartridges issued to them. On the Reservation they were allowed only four or five each, as cartridges passed as currency at twenty-five cents each and the temptation to sell or gamble them was great. I kept a thousand rounds in my tent.

As I entered the tent, Perico, second sergeant (Geronimo's half-brother), and two scouts from the rear rank slipped out of the lines and were instantly lost to sight in the brush surrounding the camp. I learned later that the three had been ordered by Geronimo to kill Chato and me. That they did not do so was due probably to a precaution I took.

How many of the Indians were leaving I did not know; nor could I even guess what effect the outbreak would have on the loyalty of my scouts, the blood relatives of the malcontents. So far as I had any means of judging, at least half would prove loyal, but there was no telling what the other half might do. That some would join in the outbreak was almost a certainty and I expected them to show their hands immediately after the issue of cartridges, but they might do so before. To enter my tent and light my lamp would make me an easy mark for any pothunters who desired to get me.

Three men I knew I could rely on absolutely—Chato,

Charley, third sergeant, and Dutchy. Dutchy, who was now a corporal, had taken a position a little to the left of the company. I had the company ground arms (stand with their rifle butts on the ground). Chato and Charley took station on either side of the door to my tent with their rifles at a ready and orders to shoot the first man who raised his gun from the ground. As I entered my tent to light my lamp the three pothunters concluded that it was a bad day for ducks and slipped out of the ranks and disappeared.

First and last, during the Geronimo campaign, over five hundred Apache, including nearly one hundred Warm Springs and Chiricahua, were enlisted as scouts. These three who deserted that night were the only ones who proved unfaithful to their trust; and some excuse might be made for them on account of the pressure brought to bear on them by their blood relatives, Geronimo and Chihuahua.

With the troops from Fort Apache we marched all night, my scouts and a dozen of Gatewood's White Mountain following the trail, a slow proceeding at night. A little after sunrise the following morning we came out on the crest of a ridge bordering a valley some fifteen or twenty miles wide. In the distance, on the opposite side of the valley, we could see the dust raised by the Indian ponies ascending another ridge.

Realizing that further pursuit by troops was useless and that we were in for a long campaign in Mexico, I reported to Captain Smith in command of the troops that I would return with my scouts to Fort Apache and wire the General again, asking for instructions.

Immediately on reaching Fort Apache I had all the Chiricahua and Warm Springs brought to my camp and counted them. Thirty-five men, eight tagged boys (those old enough to bear arms), and 101 women and children were missing.

Under the General's orders I enlisted a hundred more scouts, half of them Chiricahua, Warm Springs, and White Mountain, the other half San Carlos, Tonto, Yuma, and Mohave sent me by Captain Pierce. With a pack train of supplies I again took the field.

The leaders who took part in the outbreak were Geronimo, Chihuahua, Nachite, Mangus, and old Nana. Chato, Benito, Loco, and Zele with three-fourths of the Chiricahua and Warm Springs refused to take part in it. Almost immediately after they left their camps dissension cropped out among the hostiles. Nachite and Chihuahua charged Geronimo and Mangus with having lied to them to get them to leave by telling them that Chato and I had been killed and that troops were coming to arrest all the Chiricahua and Warm Springs and send them away. Nachite and Chihuahua threatened to kill Geronimo. This caused a split in the camps. Mangus and his small band left at once for Mexico and never rejoined the others. Chihuahua and his band stopped in the Mongollon Mountains northeast of Morenci, Arizona, uncertain whether to go on to Mexico or return to the Reservation.

Coming out with my scouts the second time, about ten days after the outbreak, I ran into Chihuahua's party. We opened fire on them at a distance of six or seven hundred yards but the hundred or so shots exchanged with them did no damage other than causing them to lose the breakfast of a fat cow they were preparing. The meat was hot on the coals when we got their camp, and was appreciated by us, as we had had no breakfast. We captured also half a dozen ponies and a little camp plunder they left in their haste to be on their way to Mexico.

We surprised Chihuahua's camp a little before sunrise and followed the trail to the Gila River Crossing about nine o'clock at night, where we camped, as our pack mules and the scouts were tired out. The hostiles were now well mounted on horses stolen from American ranches in addition to the ponies they took with them. I had with me now, besides the scouts under Chato, only Mickey Free. Bowman, I had sent back to San Carlos.

As soon as we took the field my scouts had rubbed dirt on their clean, white cotton clothes and red headbands, to render themselves as invisible as possible; but the keen eyes of Chihuahua's lookouts had discovered us nevertheless at a distance of nearly a mile, although we kept to cover as much as possible. We ascertained later that the hostiles traveled ninety miles without a halt for any purpose and did not make a camp until they reached the Mexican border. On the trail that day we found two dead babies, newly born.

At Cajon Bonita (Skeleton Cañon) Captain Hatfield, Troop D, Fourth Cavalry, had left a sergeant and seven men with his camp outfit, three wagons, tents, etc., and forty horses and mules. Chihuahua surprised the camp, killed the sergeant and two of the men, drove off the horses and mules, and burned the wagons and such camp stuff as the Indians did not want. The other men escaped.

Much to my delight, a little north of Cajon Bonita I met Crawford with Kendall's troop of the Sixth Cavalry, Lieutenant C. P. Elliott, who had been with us at San Carlos, and a dozen Mescalero scouts. Crawford was waiting for me with a telegram from the General directing the consolidation of our two commands and advising us that Sieber with another pack train was on his way to join us. The Mescalero scouts were sent back to their Reservation.

Our hundred and thirty scouts, the troop of cavalry (about forty men), and the two pack trains made quite an impressive sight, strung out along the trail. Sieber could not resist his little joke. Just as we crossed the Mexican-American border the scouts killed two bears. Sieber was riding at the head of the leading pack train. In this train was a mule we called Leppy, the largest mule in the train, who had made good her right to the place next to old Tom, the white bell horse. Leppy carried the cook's boxes. Any mule attempting to take that place next to Tom on the march was in for a bad few minutes. Sieber took Leppy out of the train, had some of the packers skin the bears, put the fresh skins on Leppy and turned her loose.

If there is anything that will frighten a mule it is the smell of blood, and the smell of a bear will set him wild. By the time Leppy was loaded both trains had passed. Crawford with the troop of cavalry was far in advance, I bringing up the rear with some of my scouts. With a snort and a bawl, Leppy started to regain her place at the head of the leading pack train, the bearskins flopping from side to side and splashing blood and bear smell on the packs of the other mules as she brushed them out of her way. In less time than it takes to tell it the plain was full of bawling, crazed mules, running in every direction, frantically trying, and many succeeding, to get rid of their packs and that awful smell. Fortunately we were in a flat, treeless country or Sieber's little joke would have been a disaster. It was bad enough as it was. Thirty or more of the mules scattered their packs all over the plain, and swearing, sweating packers were employed for hours recovering them and their cargoes. Some of them did not get into camp until nine or ten o'clock that night. Leppy was caught and the bearskins thrown away, but for two or three days thereafter a mule would suddenly start bawling and running, demoralizing half the train. The delay of the trains getting into camp brought the cause to Crawford's knowledge and what he said to Sieber cured him of any more pack train jokes.

Scouting along the crest of the Sierra Madre Mountains, approximately over the trail by which the General had come out in 1883, revealed no signs of hostiles having passed that way, and on June 20 we camped about twelve miles east of the town of Bavispe, on the headwaters of a small stream that feeds the Bavispe river a little below the town itself.

As we were making camp a Mexican came to Crawford with an invitation to visit his camp, half a mile downstream from ours and have *un tragito de vino* (a sip of wine). To our surprise the sip of wine turned out to be a drink of mescal, and the Mexican's camp was a distillery for this (in Mexico) famous liquor. A party of several Mexicans from Bavispe were having a jolly good time and welcomed us most affectionately with embraces and thanks for coming after the hostiles, who had as yet done no damage to their town.

For the uninitiated I will explain that mescal is a colorless liquor brewed from the baked heads of a species of maguey common in the desert country of northwestern Mexico. These heads, stripped of their leaves, are from six inches to twelve or fifteen inches in diameter when sufficiently mature to harvest. They are baked in a pit, the bottom of which is lined with cobblestones, and when baked develop saccharine matter so sweet that it is cloying to the taste of a person unaccustomed to it. The Indians frequently prepare and use it as a substitute for other sweets; among the Mexicans it is often retailed by old women in the little plazas of the towns as though it were candy.

Distilled, the liquor is as colorless as water but exceeds in alcoholic strength our highest proof whiskeys. The Sonorans drink it almost as though it were what they call it, *vino del pais* (country wine), but it is hardly a plaything for an amateur. To make it a little more attractive in appearance it is frequently colored by dropping orange peel or a piece of raw chicken into the keg, which is then stored for several months. This gives it a rich yellow color, indicative of great age.

Our Mexican friends, using a half of a gourd for a cup, passed around a loving cup of the fiery stuff hot from the still. A sip for me was sufficient, and that followed promptly by a swallow of water. On account of the excessive heat, a hundred and twenty or so in the shade, we had with us a couple of canteens of water from a cool little spring at our camp. As we were taking leave the Mexicans insisted on another *tragito* (swallow) all around. Without my knowing it. Sieber had emptied one of the canteens of water and filled it with mescal from a keg in the room. When I reached for the canteen of water to quench the fire in my throat he handed me the canteen of mescal and I got two big gulps of the liquor down before I realized what he had done. Subsequent proceedings interested me no more and I made a beeline for camp and my roll of bedding.

Our route for the next two days was up the east bend of the Bavispe through the towns of Bacerac, Estancia, and Guachinera. Finding no signs of hostiles in the vicinity of any of these towns, we crossed the mountain range in the bend of the Bavispe and came to the river again a little below the town of Oputo.

When I would ride into one of these towns the entire population would turn out and surround me. Usually only the men at first, then soon a woman or two would gain courage to come out, then the children. On one occasion I had explained to the Presidente with difficulty in my pigeon Mexican our mission in the country. He invited me to his office out of the sun while awaiting the arrival of the command. His clerk accompanied us. The Presidente went to the *cantina* for the inevitable gourd of mescal. His clerk then turned to me and in perfect English asked my name and inquired what state I came from. In my mortification I could have shot him! He had stood there in the plaza and let me stumble along for fifteen minutes murdering the Spanish language and had said never a word.

He was an ex-Confederate soldier—I rather suspect an ex-guerrilla, as he was very reticent about his service in the war—who with three companions had started west after the close of war. They had separated, and he had made his way to this remote town in Sonora twenty years before. Here he had married a Mexican woman and was now a grandfather. To all outward appearances he was a Mexican of the Mexicans.

In the little chapel of this same town there were some oil paintings of the saints, the Madonna, and other religious characters, that to me appeared to be unusually good. In the memory of the older inhabitants there had also been a rail of solid silver around the altar and a solid silver service for the priest. These had disappeared during the various revolutions; and when I again visited the town several years later the best of the paintings had followed suit.

Chapter X

Mexicans sell mescal to scouts. A narrow escape. A scout killed and one wounded. Scouts threaten reprisals. Cause of tragedy. Hostiles near. Martial array at Oputo. Capture of Chihuahua's women and children. Big Dave's wound. Captives sent to border. Poverty of Mexican towns. Penole y panoche. *Toyopa. Difficult scouting. "I don't fight Mexicans with cartridges."*

NOTWITHSTANDING our earnest requests of the citizens of the Mexican towns some of the scouts got mescal the night before we crossed the river at Oputo and the next day ten or a dozen of them were still under the influence of it. Fortunately they caused no disturbance, but on the trail that day several became very sick in the terrific heat and were disposed to lag behind, or get off into the brush for a nap. This was a dangerous proceeding, as the people of the half dozen small towns scattered along the river at intervals of eight or ten miles were not fully advised of our presence in the country, and a lone Indian might be mistaken for a hostile. With five or six sober scouts I remained behind the command to round up these stragglers and force them to keep moving.

There were, of course, no telegraph lines, and communication between the towns even by mail or courier was irregular and at long intervals. The people had not yet recovered from the fear of the Apache, and this fear was enhanced by the occasional raids of cattle thieves from the United States, as merciless as the Apache themselves.

Our trail for the day led up the dry, sandy bed of a wide cañon that entered the river from the west. There was no grass for our animals along the bed of the Bavispe and our Indian guides had told us that we would get both grass and a cool spring of water near the head of the cañon. This we found to be true, but it was not the end of our troubles; only the beginning.

On my way up the cañon, with the command far ahead and only four or five of my scouts for company, I suddenly heard the report of a gun, the whistle of the bullet, and my broad-brim Texas hat jerked back on my head. The shot came from a bush beside the road, and in another minute my scouts had the worst frightened man I ever saw. He was a Mexican farmer and clinging to him was a little lad about six or seven years of age, moaning in terror. With a scout holding each of his arms and the other scouts covering him with their rifles the man stood actually paralyzed with fright. His gun had dropped at his feet. The child, when I patted his head and put my arm around his shoulder, recovered from the fright the quicker of the two. The man was still in a semi-daze when ten or fifteen minutes later I was able to convince him that he was free to go to his home. He moved off down the trail, looking back every step or so, in the evident expectation that it was only a piece of cruel sport to shoot him at our leisure.

A rather sad picture; but picture to yourself what it would have been had my scouts been really hostiles! And it was not altogether without its serious side for me. There was a neat little piece missing from the brim of my hat just above my nose.

When the man had partly recovered from his fright he explained in incoherent sentences that his gun, an antiquated Sharps rifle, had gone off accidentally. He and his boy were rabbit hunting with the rifle at full cock in expectation of jumping a rabbit any moment. Then they saw the Indians with the command and hid in the bush where we found them. They were too frightened to see anything but Apache; even the mounted troops and the packers were mounted Apache. When the command had passed they remained in the bush just long enough to come out as I passed by with my rear guard. In their haste to seek cover again the trigger of the rifle had caught on a twig.

In a heat that our surgeon pronounced 128° in the shade of a tree, and the rest of us pronounced at least a hundred degrees hotter, we were making camp at sundown when a commotion started in the scout camp, across the little stream from ours. Crawford, Sieber, and I ran over to see what was the matter. Two of our scouts were just coming in, one wounded and weak from loss of blood, the other supporting him and carrying their rifles. The wounded man had been shot through the arm. Back on the trail five or six miles, they said, was another scout, dead. A Mexican had fired on them from the brush without provocation; in fact, they had not seen him either before or after he had shot, as he had immediately mounted a mule and fled.

Hell, or at least the threat of it, broke loose in the scout camp. Thirty or forty of the scouts immediately stripped for battle and started for Oputo, about twelve miles away, determined on killing any Mexicans they could find. The people of the town did not as yet know that Indians of any sort were in the vicinity, as we had crossed the river some distance below the town without meeting any of the townspeople. It was only with the greatest difficulty that we induced the scouts to stop, return to the camp, and listen to us.

All night long we argued the matter with them. Nine-tenths of them were for returning to the United States at once, killing any Mexicans they might meet *en route*. The Indian who had been killed and the wounded one were of the White Mountain tribe, and their fellow tribesmen were the hardest by far to deal with. A notable fact, however, was that the Chiricahua and Warm Springs were the least excited. The San Carlos, Yuma, and Mohave were in a panic of fright, arguing that the Mexicans would kill them all if we did not get out of the country at once. Back to the Reservation for them that night if their lives were to be saved!

The arguments of Chato and one or two influential White Mountain, added to our persuasions, finally prevailed and it was agreed that all would remain in camp until we could find out why the scouts had been fired on. We were satisfied that a mistake had been made and hoped we could clear the matter up to the satisfaction of all concerned.

At daylight I went back to bury the dead scout. I took with me six or eight of the least excited of the scouts, with Chato in charge of them. Shortly after I left the camp, three of the dead man's personal friends or relatives followed me without Crawford's knowledge. They kept behind me out of sight until they saw us pick up the dead man, then set out for the Mexican town.

What their object was I never knew, but it is a safe bet that some Mexican was playing in big luck that they did not meet him before they came upon a sign I will mention presently that diverted their attention.

An examination of the ground near the dead man,

coupled with what the survivors had told us, made the cause of the tragedy clear and did much to allay the anger of his friends and relatives.

The dead man, we had been told, was one of those who had been drunk the night before and was so sick that he was hidden in some bushes by his two friends until I had passed by. When he had partially recovered they, one on either side, were assisting him to camp. Suddenly a shot was fired and he sank down mortally wounded. Almost instantly a second shot followed, breaking the arm of the scout on the dead man's left and causing him to drop his rifle, which his companion picked up as the two of them took to cover in a bush nearby. After waiting a while with no further shots following, they retreated to the side of the cañon opposite to that from which the shots had come and made their way to camp.

At the point where the tragedy had occurred the cañon was a big dry wash, about a quarter of a mile in width. Just at this point a smaller cañon entered it from the north. About seventy-five yards up this cañon was the track of a small mule that had evidently stopped on reaching the edge of the large cañon up which the command had passed, then turned back into the brush bordering the large cañon and continued down toward the Bavispe river and the Mexican settlements.

Behind a bush at the point where the mule had stopped there were the imprints of a man's shoe and of his knee, where he had knelt to fire the two shots. Two empty shells proved the gun to have been a Winchester and accounted for the short interval between the shots. Some years later I met the other actor in the little tragedy, an American, and found in him all that one could desire in a friend. So far from blaming him, I could but admire his courage in tackling three well-armed Apache, not knowing how many more there might be in the vicinity.

He explained that he had been on a visit to one of his ranches and was returning down the small cañon when he saw the three scouts and thought them hostiles. He had not seen the command or me, as we had passed some little time before.

We had just finished burying the dead scout when his three relatives who had followed us came back from the direction of Oputo with the information that near Oputo they had struck the trail of some hostiles who had been in the outskirts of the town the night before, and had evidently driven off a band of horses. There were three moccasin tracks behind the horses; and the trail, which the scouts had followed a little distance, led toward the mountains east of the Bavispe river.

Here was double good fortune: it raised a doubt whether the scout had not been killed by a hostile, at least it gave us that chance for an argument, as the surviving scouts had not seen their assailant; and it offered a probable chance for a scrap and some legitimate blood-letting; very desirable when a crowd of half-crazed men are determined to kill someone. Returning to camp at once with my news, the command was assembled and we started for Oputo to pick up the trail.

As we moved out of camp, some of the White Mountain scouts scattered through the hills and we heard the sound of firing in the direction they had taken. Investigation revealed that the dead man's relatives were "taking it out" on Mexican cattle. They must have killed a score or two, but we thought it best not to interfere. A hundred dollars would cover the damage. Cheap at the price for what might have happened; but the Mexicans later refused payment, as well they might in view of what followed.

When I entered Oputo all the able-bodied men of the town, some thirty-five or forty in number, were lined up in front of the principal *cantina* (saloon) ready to take the warpath. They were armed with every conceivable type of antiquated firearm, aged cap and ball horse pistols, muzzle-loading, single-barrel shotguns; these, with a few Sharps rifles that had seen better days, made up the major part of the arsenal. Here and there I noted an aged Winchester, but as the ammunition I saw for this arm appeared to be mostly refilled shells I had my doubts of the efficacy even of this, the most promising of their weapons for offense. One thing, however, was not lacking—abundant provision for Dutch courage. The *cantina* was doing a land-office business.

I was dressed in brown canvas trousers, a western (semi-cowboy) hat, and blue flannel shirt. But I carried with me, strapped to my saddle, my army blouse with the insignia of a second lieutenant of cavalry. This I always donned before entering a town. The rear of the martial array was toward me as I entered the plaza where they were assembled, and they did not see me until I rode around their flank and appeared before them. If an angel with a flaming sword had suddenly dropped from the skies he would have created no greater sensation. Apparently word had reached them that American troops were in the country, but they had not dreamed that we were so near. In a moment a shout went up: *Soldados Americanos! Soldados Americanos!*

People came pouring out of the neighboring houses, the martial line broke up into a cheering crowd of laughing, yelling men, and in a moment I was surrounded by a mass of happy people who seemed bent on hugging both my mule and me. A call was sent out for the Presidente, to whom I explained our mission. Needless to say, he accepted my suggestion that he disband his command and leave to us the task they had contemplated. On the arrival of the command we camped on the river at a little distance from the town and were flooded with such delicacies as their poor village afforded; nor would the grateful people accept a cent in payment.

Crawford prepared at once to give the hostiles a surprise. To attempt to follow the trail with our troop of cavalry and pack trains would be folly, feeling sure, as we did, that the hostiles were not very far away. The question has often been asked me why we used cumbersome and useless cavalry in these expeditions when the cavalry only retarded the movements of the scouts and hardly ever got into action against the hostiles. The answer is that the cavalry was supposed to serve as a rallying point for the scouts, increasing their morale and protecting the pack trains. The danger of inadequate protection for camp equipage and supplies was exemplified in the disaster to Hatfield's camp. The disadvantages were, however, found to outweigh the advantages and the General abandoned the use of cavalry in Crawford's and Major Davis' second expedition.

Crawford detailed about thirty scouts, under Chato and a White Mountain sergeant we called Big Dave, to take the trail of the three hostiles who had been down to the town the night before and follow it as far as they could that afternoon. They were given two days' rations and were to try the next day to reach the hostile camp and surprise it. Sieber and I wanted to go along, but

Crawford was afraid we would be an encumbrance rather than an aid and turned us down, much to our disgust. We had the satisfaction, if it was satisfaction, of having him regret later that he did not let us go.

About noon the next day, June 23, the scouts returned to camp with fifteen women and children prisoners. Among them was a little boy about four years of age with a flesh wound in his arm. Chato reported that one woman had been killed in the fight but no men. We ascertained later that one man had been shot in the leg but was carried off by his companions.

The only casualty among the scouts was Big Dave, who had been shot through the elbow, the bullet splintering the bones of both the upper and the lower arm. He was aiming at one of the hostiles when the bullet struck him. From the scouts we learned that a little after daylight, when they had taken up the trail where they had left it the night before, it was raining. The trail led up a ridge that came down from the main Sierra Madre Mountain. Suddenly the rain ceased and the sun came out from behind the cloud. On account of the rain the scouts were proceeding rather incautiously, covering their heads with their blankets. As the rain ceased they saw the hostile camp on the ridge five or six hundred yards away. At the same moment one of the hostiles came out of a brush shelter they had erected, caught sight of the scouts, and gave the alarm. The Indian men, with most of the women and children, fled up the ridge, the men stopping now and then to fire back at the scouts to delay them. It was one of these shots that had found a resting place in Big Dave's arm. Both Sieber and I felt, and Crawford now agreed with us, that had either of us been with the scouts we would have bagged the entire camp. As the detachment was constituted there was no definite commander; composed of selections from the various bands, no two bands acknowledged the same chief, and the young men got out of control and became careless at a time when they should have been most careful.

The surgeon with us, a very competent and high-class man, was for amputating Dave's arm, but the Indians would not consent to it, saying that they would cure it Indian fashion. Procuring some green twigs about the thickness of the lead in a lead pencil and some three inches long, they bent them into two circles, each the size of a dollar. These they wrapped around and through with narrow strips of cloth until the hole in the center was about the size of a dime. One of these circles they put over the hole made by the bullet when it entered and the other where the bullet had come out. Before doing this they had accepted the aid of our surgeon to the extent of removing the small pieces of splintered bone, which Dave stood stoically without anesthetics.

The small circles in place, a poultice was made of green sprigs of the *yerba de vivora* (snake root), and bound over the wounds. This dressing was removed and renewed daily the two or three days while Dave remained in camp with us. One care of the wound that particularly struck our surgeon was that no water was allowed to touch it. This, he said, was a knowledge he would not have supposed the Indians to possess. He was still insistent that Dave's arm would stiffen and he would have little or no use of it; but when I saw Dave at Fort Apache three months later he had recovered the use of his arm and of all the fingers of that hand except two, and these he said would recover.

The small child's wound was a simple flesh wound in the upper arm. This the Indians left to our surgeon, evidently thinking little of it.

The captives and our two wounded, Dave and the man wounded by the civilian, having been sent back to the border, we resumed our scouting operations, following the mountain range in the bend of the Bavispe as far south as its confluence with the Rio Aros, where the two form the Yaqui.

The small Mexican towns through which we passed were the poorest communities I have ever seen. We were hungry for anything in the nature of vegetables, but my inquiries for food of any sort were almost always met with a refusal to sell even the little chili (dried red pepper) they had, as it was needed for the townspeople. This with beans, meat, and mescal comprised the only food in most of the villages. In the hills were hundreds of wild cattle which the owners had abandoned on account of the Apache. Anyone was free to kill them and we even took advantage of this condition to gain relief occasionally from the eternal bacon.

One food new to us they sometimes had that met with our immediate approval and was purchased whenever we could induce them to sell it, or could get some woman to prepare the principal ingredient for us. To our untutored ears it was *pinoly-pinoch,* to the Mexicans it was *penole y panoche.* Penole was small grain parched and ground fine on a flat stone, a round stone being used as a grinder—such as had been the custom at the birth of Christianity and for ages before. A small-grained native corn was used when obtainable; lacking that, wheat, barley, the seed of the sugar cane, or any edible grain was substituted.

Panoche was crude, brown, Mexican homemade sugar, molded in small molds about the size of a teacup. A heaping teaspoonful of penole in a pint of water, a chunk of panoche, the size you could bite off, a twig to stir the mixture, and you had a lunch that would stay with you the hardest day in the mountains. The Taharumarah Indians of western Chihuahua are credited with almost incredible feats of speed and endurance in the mountains with no food but this to sustain them. An English friend of mine once told me that this was essentially the same food that sustained the Scotch Highlanders when they were fighting the English in centuries past.

But the villagers were not without local pride. One of their boasts amused me, until it became monotonous. Discouraged with my efforts to buy something in the way of fresh food I would usually wind up my inquiries with the question, "Is there *anything* you have?" and the invariable reply would be:

"Pues, Señor, tenemos muy buen agua, la mejor en la sierra." (Well, sir, we have mighty good water, the best in the mountains.)

As the water of all the towns was identically the same, that from the Bavispe River, the boast finally lost its significance.

In the little town of Nacori I met a curious state of affairs. The population was 313 souls; but of these only fifteen were adult males. Every family had lost one or more male members at the hands of the Apache.

Here also I first heard the legend of Toyopa. This mine was said to have been of such wonderful richness that blocks of silver taken from it had to be cut into several pieces so that mules could carry them to the seacoast for shipment to Spain. My informant, the white-haired Presidente, a man over eighty years of age, told me that his grandfather, who also had lived to be a very old man, had worked in the mine as a boy, and that it was in a mountain range the Presidente pointed out to the east of Nacori.

The Apache attacked the place one day when the men were nearly all away at a fiesta in one of the river towns, killed everyone in the camp, destroyed the buildings, and blew up the entrance to the mine. A hundred years went by with no force in the country strong enough to conquer the Apache and the mine had never been found.

Those who would seek, as have hundreds before them, the lost mine of Toyopa, should bear in mind the statement of the old Presidente's grandfather: "Here in Nacori, where we stand, on a still night one could hear the dogs bark and the church bell ring in Toyopa."

On the trail a few days after we left Nacori two Chiricahua scouts took a detour and came into camp later with several bars of silver. But I am sure they were not from Toyopa. Some Mexican with his face turned to Heaven had yielded them up, and they had been cached until opportunity offered to recover them. Our coming into old Apache stamping ground had afforded the opportunity and the scouts had profited.

Man should be thankful that the future is a closed book! How it would have saddened our hearts to have foreseen that thirty miles east of Nacori we were passing over the spot where Crawford, six months later, was to meet his death at the hands of the very Mexicans whose lives he was protecting from the Apache!

Finding no sign of hostiles in the vicinity of Nacori, we moved north again along the Bavispe River bottom until Crawford decided to try the main Sierra Madre range to the east of us. Another expedition, similarly constituted of a small troop of cavalry, a pack train, and about thirty Apache scouts, was now in Mexico and supposed to be operating east of us; the whole under Major Wirt Davis, with Lieutenant M. W. Day in command of the scouts; but we had seen nothing of them.

Climbing to the crest of the Sierra Madre was no picnic. It took two days from daylight to dark each day. Mules fell and rolled down the mountain slopes, killing themselves and destroying their loads. Most of the mule fatalities occurred among some northern mules, too large for mountain work. These had been brought down from Nebraska and had reached us as we were waiting for Sieber and his pack train.

Our small southwestern mule, a cross with the Mexican jack, was far better in the mountains and exhibited almost human intelligence. More than once I have seen them size up a passageway between trees, decide it was too narrow for their packs, and go around it; finding that a pack touched a low limb they would squat and get under it, or turn back and take another way around. Sometimes they would fall and roll a hundred yards or more down a mountain slope, get up, climb back to the trail, and join the train again as though nothing had happened. Such a fall invariably killed the larger mules or crippled them so badly they had to be destroyed.

With my introduction to the slopes of these mountains I recalled the talk I had had with Geronimo that critical night at Sulphur Springs:

"I don't fight Mexicans with cartridges. I fight them with rocks and keep my cartridges to fight the white soldiers."

At the time I thought he was having fun with me or trying to dodge my request; but now on these steep mountain slopes I could see what he meant and appreciate the effectiveness of his rock ammunition.

The Indians would raid a Mexican village; troops, regulars or irregulars, would follow the trail, which invariably led them up a steep mountainside. The Indians, above them, would scatter along the ridge and at the opportune moment each Indian would loosen as large a boulder as he could manage and start it down the slope. As they crashed down the steep mountainside, other boulders were loosened and joined their fellows, until the whole slope seemed in motion as from an earthquake. Trees the thickness of a man's leg would be smashed to kindling. The Mexican force on the trail below was out of luck unless it was warned in time to retreat.

A week on the crest and eastern slopes of the Sierra Madre brought no results except to exhaust our rations. Returning to the range of hills in the bend of the Bavispe, where there was much better grass than on the main mountain, we went into camp and sent the trains back for more supplies. During the two weeks' wait for the return of the trains Sieber and I with a dozen or fifteen scouts went south again to the Aros River above its junction with the Bavispe. Here we sent some of the scouts as far south of the Aros as they would go in fear of meeting Mexican troops, but no trail of the hostiles was found. A year later, however, we learned that our guess had been good. Mangus and his small band were even then south of the Aros, but thirty or forty miles east of where we had crossed it.

Chapter XI

Meeting with Day. "Elephantitus." Day's capture. Scouts kill two hostiles. I take trail of Geronimo's band. Horse meat and berries. Difficult trailing. The Apache stronghold. "No time for an amateur." Capture of Elliott by Mexican troops. Startled Mexican officers. Geronimo gets fresh horses. I meet Mexican troops. Kindness of Lord Beresford. Mexican commander at Paso del Norte (Juarez) pronounces us outlaws. I resign from the army.

WITH the return of the pack trains, the large mules were replaced by small ones, and we were ready for the field again. During my absence on the Aros, Crawford had sent scouts over all the country within fifty miles of his camp, but no trails other than cattle trails or those between the towns had been discovered. He decided to return to the main Sierra Madre and scout it more thoroughly. Those of Chihuahua's party who had escaped from the scouts had fled toward the east and must be somewhere in the main Sierra.

Ascending its western slope, early one morning we came upon the trail of a party of hostiles. In a few miles it was joined by a trail our scouts pronounced the trail of a scouting party in pursuit—evidently from Major Wirt Davis' command.

About nine o'clock I rode into a little glade beside a small stream and saw two Americans seated on the ground with their feet on a log in front of them. They were in their undershirts and torn overalls; hatless, dirty, unshaven for weeks, their feet swathed in bandages made from their flannel shirts. Around them were some thirty armed Apache with whom my scouts began at once to fraternize.

"Hi there!" called one of the scarecrows, "Are you Davis?"

"Yes," I replied, "but who the hell are you?"

"I'm Day. Got anything to smoke and eat?"

I had, and a small flask of mescal as well. While they were eating my lunch I got from them a tale of the nerviest piece of work of which I have ever had personal knowledge.

Three days before, their command had struck the trail of Geronimo's band. Realizing that it would be folly to attempt to catch the hostiles with the pack train and soldiers, Major Davis had sent Day and the scouts ahead on the chance of locating them and holding them until the troop of cavalry could come up. But the hostiles were farther away than Major Davis calculated, and Day and his scouts kept going.

They had started with just a lunch, which they had eaten the first day. In order to travel better with the scouts, Day and his chief of scouts (whose name I have unfortunately forgotten) discarded their shoes for moccasins. Almost immediately after leaving the command rain set in and the moccasins, soaked with water, became useless. They took them off and for three days had gone barefoot over the sharp rocks and through the cactus-infested slopes of the mountains. Their feet swelled to almost twice their normal size, but they kept up with the scouts by tearing their shirts to pieces and using them for bandages. When our surgeon removed the bandages their toes were hardly distinguishable. A good example of "elephantitus of the feet" he pronounced it.

Late in the afternoon of the third day, where they were now camped, they had overtaken Geronimo and his band, but with no better luck than our scouts had had. They had killed a woman and a boy about fifteen years of age and captured fifteen women and children. The men and the rest of the women and children had escaped up the mountain ridge on which they had been in camp. This was the usual result in fights with the Apache. Whenever they camped in fear of possible pursuit they always chose a place where it was practically impossible to surprise them, and where in case of attack they had an easy line of escape in their rear.

The scouts had had better luck a couple of weeks earlier when they had ambushed and killed two of the hostiles in Sierra La Hoya (Mountain of the Hole) some miles farther north. The scouts were operating alone and away from the command at the time.

Crawford was of the opinion that those of Geronimo's band who had escaped from Day, with but three or four ponies and practically no food, clothing, or camp equipage, would move north or south to raid one of the Sonora towns on the Bavispe River. Having proved the utter futility of hunting the Apache with cavalry and a pack train, and profiting by the lesson learned when the scouts were allowed to go out alone, he ordered Sieber and me to take up Geronimo's trail with Chato, Mickey, and about forty picked scouts. Five pack mules loaded with three days' rations, the belongings of the scouts and ourselves, extra ammunition, etc., under the care of two packers and a night herder accompanied us. The three days' rations were to last us six days, at the end of which time we were to rejoin the command. That was forty-three years ago and I have not yet rejoined it; which I think is a record for a long fast.

The rainy season had set in some two months before and we were soaked to the skin every day, and at night no better off, for the driving deluge had penetrated the canvas covers for our bedding. We had brought no tents with the command, only canvas covers for our blankets and for the pack-train cargo. Thinking I would have no use for my army blouse until I rejoined the command, I left it with Crawford, substituting a six-foot strip of canvas with a slit for my head as a better protection from the rain. I was thus without any insignia whatever, a circumstance that caused me a bad quarter of an hour some weeks later. My brown canvas trousers, torn to shreds, had been replaced by a pair of black civilian trousers that by chance I had in my pack.

The officers on Indian duty, following the General's example, all rode mules. In the mountains, especially, they were far superior to any horse that was ever foaled; surer footed, more enduring, less likely to stray, and able to sustain themselves on grass that would soon put a horse down and out, they were the only things for the duty we were on. My mule was a sturdy, courageous Missouri citizen who carried me as though I were a race-track jockey. He had but one defect—he was a very light gray, easily distinguishable at a great distance in this drab country. For the sake of less visibility I left him with the command and took a mouse-colored mule instead.

On August 8, the day following Day's fight with Geronimo, we took the trail of the four or five animals the hostiles still possessed. One of these was a shod mule, the others all small, barefooted Mexican ponies. But for the mule we could never have followed the trail. The hard rains obliterated the light tracks of the ponies, but the mule's small, shod feet sank into the ground and made a more distinct mark. As the days passed, one by one the ponies gave out and were killed by the hostiles for food. The last two or three days of our trailing was of the mule alone, the only survivor; and he finally lost three of his shoes.

Contrary to Crawford's expectations Geronimo moved due east, heading for the eastern Chihuahua slopes of the Sierra; bent evidently on raiding a Chihuahua town or ranch rather than one in Sonora. When our rations gave out we kept on, hoping to overtake the hostiles before they got a remount. Our rations exhausted, we lived on the flesh of the ponies the hostiles had killed and such roots, berries, etc., as the country afforded and the scouts knew to be edible. On one lucky occasion we caught several young turkeys. There were plenty of deer in the mountains but we could not shoot for fear of alarming the hostiles, whom we might overtake any time.

One of the scouts, a Yuma corporal we called Rowdy, who spoke quite good English, was very indignant at our eating horses and refused to join in the feast.

"Him poor horse, work fo' you alla day. No much get eat in mountain. Cally you all day. Fall down; you kill, eat. Damn! No good."

But our hungry stomachs had no ears.

Our progress was necessarily slow. The hostiles frequently changed direction to confuse anyone who might be following them. The trail would at times lead due north, switch to the east, bend back toward the west, or turn south. Frequently it would change direction on rocky ground, where even the tracks of the mule did not show. In such cases a halt, often of an hour or more, would be necessary to enable the scouts to again find the trail. These tactics, coupled with detours to avoid natural barriers in this mountainous country, forced us to travel a hundred and forty or fifty miles to cover a hundred as the crow flies.

In crossing the Sierra Madre from Nacori in Sonora to El Valle de San Buena Ventura in Chihuahua I passed through what the Apache had considered an impenetrable stronghold until General Crook brought consternation to them by invading it in the spring of 1883. For a generation past, since the early days of Cochise, Mangus Colorado, and Delgadito, they had defended it against every attempt of the Mexicans to take it. And it was well worth defending. Here I got my first clear comprehension of the life these people led before civilization clamped its shackles on them. And I must say that I envied them that life.

The uplands of the Sierra Madre, with an elevation of some seven to nine thousand feet, are a succession of little glades in the pine timber; level as a floor, one or two miles in diameter, knee deep in grass, and the sources of little ice-cold streams that, on the western slope, fall in cataracts over the escarpment to form the rivers of Sonora thousands of feet below. In these glades the Apache made his home from early spring to late fall, when snow would drive him to the lowlands of Sonora to the west or Chihuahua to the east.

The Sonora slopes I have described, an impassable barrier to the Mexican troops, regulars or irregulars, who attempted them. Toward the east the slopes were more gradual, falling off gently to the Chihuahua plains with an occasional small range of hills intervening. Attacks on their stronghold from the east were not feared, as the western part of Chihuahua was sparsely settled and the distance to the larger cities great. The officials of the cities had troubles of their own, and the pioneer villages were allowed to take care of themselves.

Here, for nine months of the year, the Indian lived in a climate that but for intermittent rains during six weeks of midsummer was ideal. Food, such as he was accustomed to, was abundant, and free for the taking. Acorns, roots, berries in season, herbs known as edible, the women and children gathered. Meat, his principal sustenance, was sport to procure as the hills were alive with deer and the lower slopes with antelope. The animals killed for food provided him with clothing and cover for his hut.

Every day was a holiday. Foot races, pony races, dances, and gambling, for the Indian was an inveterate gambler, whiled away the time. And if some lucky gambler cleaned up the bunch, there was the most exciting of all amusements to fall back upon and replenish the exchequer—a raid on one of the Mexican towns. That the Indians considered these raids in the light of an exciting adventure rather than as a dangerous undertaking is proved by the fact that the Indian would never keep the peace. Repeatedly, he made peace with the inhabitants of the Sonora or Chihuahua towns; frequently he would be at peace with one town and at war with another a day's journey away. Tomorrow, conditions might be reversed. He could at any time have made a lasting peace with the Mexicans, actually of Indian blood themselves, who would have been glad to keep it on their part, permitting the Apache to live among them and become absorbed in semicivilized life. When I first went to Coralitos there were four full-blood Apache, two men and two women, living there, intermarried with Mexicans. And such was the case in other Mexican towns.

But the Apache's only interest in the "man with a hoe" was as the source of supply for things he craved and nature did not provide. When he craved these things, or felt the need of excitement more strenuous than his mountain home offered, a party was made up. This might include four or five, or several times that number, of the young men under the leadership of a chief, a subchief, or of a man who, like Geronimo, had won distinction as a leader. The number in the party depended on the magnitude of the raid contemplated and what it was proposed to bring back. If the object sought was a sizable herd of cattle or a large band of horses, or if the raid was to be an extended one, such as a raid into American territory where stout opposition might be encountered, the larger number took part.

If a village or ranch in Chihuahua or Sonora was selected for tribute, it was a matter of only a couple of days on their ponies to reach it. With only a woman or two as cooks to encumber them they could cover much ground in a very short time, and they were so familiar with the country that night impeded them hardly more than day. Returning with their loot, a rear guard was thrown back to retard pursuit. The Mexicans were so fearful of ambush that they seldom penetrated even the foothills of the main Sierra, abandoning the chase before reaching them.

The Apache, so far as I have been able to trace their history, were never scalp hunters for the honor of accumulating a number of scalps, as were most of our plains

Indians. In fact, after General Crook subdued them in 1872-73 they abandoned scalping entirely, except possibly in one or two isolated instances of which I have no record or authentic report.

Nor was the Apache a sneak thief. What he took, he took in open warfare. In my nearly four years among them neither I nor anyone within my knowledge was ever the victim of petty pilfering, although opportunities were abundant.

But it was not always war with the Mexicans. Frequently large bands of the Indians, or even the entire Chiricahua and Warm Springs tribes, would patch up a peace with the authorities of the small towns and camp near them for weeks or months at a stretch, trading to the citizens of Chihuahua ponies and other loot collected in Sonora; or reversing the process if the town was in Sonora.

The principal articles of barter which the Indians craved and could not obtain in their mountain homes were tobacco and mescal, both products of the hot lowlands of Sonora and Sinaloa and mediums of exchange with the neighboring states of Chihuahua and Durango. Bartering for mescal was not entirely devoid of risk for the Indian. On more than one occasion a mescal drunk in a friendly town had afforded opportunity to the citizens of the town to add a few good Indians to their score. Such a breach of hospitality would, of course, be resented by the Indians and war with that town would follow until the matter was forgotten, or an equivalent number of Mexicans had been cut off in their prime. These affiliations with the Mexicans usually took place in the winter months, when the Indians were driven from the mountains by snow.

I was an inveterate cigarette smoker, and having exhausted the small package of tobacco I had brought with me I was suffering for a smoke. On the trail one day I happened to see Sieber take from his pocket part of a plug of chewing tobacco, bite off a piece, and return the plug to its retreat. Recalling to mind that in my boyhood days I had occasionally tried the weed in that form, I suggested to Sieber that a chew might satisfy my craving. With no show of enthusiasm he passed the plug over.

I found the result so satisfactory that later in the day I suggested another helping. His reaction to the request was not what you might call hilarious, and he did not pass over the plug. Taking his knife from his pocket, he cut off a piece you could put in a thimble, passed it to me, and securely retrenched the plug in a back pocket of his overalls, which he ostentatiously buttoned up. For a little distance we rode on in silence, but Sieber was thinking. Presently he spurred his mule up beside mine and unburdened his mind.

"Lieutenant," he said, "I don't want you to think that I begrudge you anything. You're welcome to most any thing I've got; but I must say, Lieutenant, that this is a damned poor time for an amateur to learn to chew."

When Crawford found that the trail led east and we did not return at the end of six days, he sent Lieutenant Elliott to overtake us with five scouts, two packers, and pack mules with three days' more rations. With a plainly marked trail to follow, Elliott was able to travel twice as fast as we had traveled.

By August 25, we had left the main Sierra Madre Mountains, crossed a minor range between the Casas Grandes and Santa Maria rivers, and were camped on the Santa Maria about twelve miles above El Valle de San Buena Ventura, the largest town in western Chihuahua. In the afternoon of that day we had come across some Mexican cattle, the first we had seen since leaving Sonora. The hostiles had killed a beef, and we enjoyed a welcome relief from our daily diet of tough horse meat. Then Puck or the Devil took a hand in our enterprise, with consequences far from pleasant.

A Mexican cowboy discovered the carcass of the steer after we had passed, and the footprints of the hostiles, now but a day ahead of us, and of my scouts. In El Valle there happened to be a force of one hundred and fifty Mexican regular troops en route from Chihuahua to Sonora. The cowboy raced to El Valle and reported the presence of a big band of hostile Apache. Joined by a hundred volunteers from the town, the troops came out to welcome the hostiles to Chihuahua.

Elliott, not realizing he was so near us, camped about four miles short of our camp and a couple of miles beyond where the hostiles had killed the beef. He and his scouts also helped themselves to a little fresh meat as they passed the remains, thus furnishing circumstantial evidence that came within an ace of causing his summary execution.

The sun was just setting when my scouts suddenly began yelling and stripping for action. Two Indians had appeared on a small knoll a quarter of a mile back on our trail and were calling to our scouts, who were now streaming over the trail back to them, shedding their clothing and loading their guns as they went. I called to Sieber asking what was the matter. He did not answer but ran to his mule and jumping on it bareback took out after the scouts, calling to them to stop. I followed suit.

Half a mile from camp we caught up with the leading scouts and succeeded in halting them. With them were the two Indians we had seen on the knoll, who turned out to be scouts we had left with Crawford. They told us that they, with Elliott, had been sent to overtake us, had camped four miles back not thinking we were so near, and had been attacked by an overwhelming force of Mexicans. The two scouts were a little way from the camp, hunting. Taking to the hills as soon as the Mexicans appeared, they had escaped; but Elliott, the other three scouts, and the two packers had been killed; the mules with their supplies, etc., had been taken by the Mexicans, and were on their way toward the Mexican town.

My scouts at once decided to pursue the Mexicans, kill as many as possible, and then start for the United States. This I vetoed, explaining that the Mexicans greatly outnumbered them and probably by the time they were overtaken would be in El Valle. The greater number suggestion made no appeal to them as they held the Mexicans in contempt, but a talk with the two surviving scouts convinced my scouts that the Mexicans were by now too far away. We decided to go on as far as the place where Elliott had camped.

It was still light enough to see when we reached the site of his camp, but we could find no remains of him, of his two packers, or of the scouts. Evidently, if they had been killed the Mexicans had carried off the bodies—a thing I thought very unlikely, and I began to doubt that the Mexicans had killed them. Returning to our own camp, I told Sieber to let none of our scouts leave it until I returned from El Valle, where I would go to see if I could find out what had happened to Elliott. If I was not back by daylight he and the scouts were to get back to the command and report to Captain Crawford.

By now it was as dark as the proverbial stack of black cats and raining hard, with frequent flashes of lightning illuminating the dim road to the town.

About halfway to town a flash of lightning showed me four mounted men approaching from the direction in which I was headed. They saw me at the same time and challenged me with a

"Quien va?" (Who goes there?)

"Amigo. Oficial del ejército Americano" (Friend. An American army officer), I replied.

In a moment we met and I found them to be two officers from the Mexican command with two soldiers as escort. I explained briefly who I was and why I was in that part of the country, and asked about Elliott. They assured me that he and the packers and scouts were unharmed, but were being detained in El Valle until their identity could be established. Their Colonel, they said, had about come to the conclusion that a mistake had been made, but Elliott could speak no Spanish and the Colonel had not yet found an interpreter when he sent these officers out to see if they could learn anything.

We had all halted when we met and were quietly sitting our animals while these explanations were being made. A flash of lightning, the snort of a horse, and an exclamation of fright from one of the soldiers caused me to glance around. In the dim afterglow of the flash I saw a sight that caused me a bad second or two until I realized what it was.

We were surrounded by ten or a dozen naked men, their black eyes flashing in their set, determined faces, upturned inquiringly. Dark bands about their heads to keep the hair from their eyes, the inevitable breech cloths and double belts of cartridges—beyond these they were as nature had sent them into the world. In an instant all was black again. One could not see ten feet away. The two officers and their two men sat as though turned to stone. I would have given a penny for their thoughts. I doubt that they even breathed for a few moments.

Then came another flash of lightning and I recognized Chato and some of my scouts. Chato afterward explained that they were determined that I should not go alone to the Mexican town for fear that I might be killed by Mexicans on the way. If I were killed they were going to take toll of those who killed me, then make their way back to Sieber and the command. They had slipped away from our camp in the darkness without Sieber's knowledge, and had followed a few yards behind me.

I assured Chato that all was well and sent two of the scouts back to tell Sieber to come down near the town the following morning to meet me. An explanation to the officers seemed to satisfy them that there was no danger to be feared, but as Chato and his men were determined to accompany us to the edge of the town, I am sure that the scalps of the Mexicans felt very loose until we got there.

The officers took me at once to the house in which their commander was quartered. I found him a fine old gentleman and greatly relieved to learn that a mistake had been made from which nothing very serious had resulted. He was already half convinced that Elliott's statement was true. In the town he had found two Americans who spoke a little Spanish. They had recently established a wagon repair shop in the town and had the confidence of the town officials. Elliott had been released in their custody. When first brought to the town he and his men had been confined under guard in a vacant adobe warehouse. With my explanation the guard was now removed, and the two packers and the three scouts were allowed to spend the night there.

My explanation of our taking some of the meat from the steer killed by the hostiles brought out the fact of our being on short rations, and the kindly old Colonel, although it was now midnight, insisted on having a feast. He ordered food prepared, sent for Elliott and some of his officers, and provided an ample supply of very good wine. The officers, educated men and a lot of good fellows, were disposed to have a little fun with us, now that everything had turned out all right. But Elliott could not see the joke in it. He told me later that about a hundred shots had been fired at them but no shots returned and only the greatest good luck had saved them from a catastrophe. He added:

"All I want now is to live to see the day when I will come down here with a saber in my hand and a troop of cavalry at my back!"

It was near noon of the following day before we could tear ourselves loose from our new friends, giving the hostiles an additional six or eight hours' start. I sent back to the command with Elliott ten of my scouts who were becoming footsore. I was not in much better shape myself, my shoes having given out, but one of the scouts had made me a new pair of soles by tying on the bottom of the shoes strips of rawhide from the slaughtered beef.

At the end of three days' travel southeast from El Valle we came out upon the crest of a small range of mountains to see, fifteen or eighteen miles ahead of us, small dots on the plain which the scouts pronounced Geronimo's band headed north. They had raided the Santa Clara ranch of General Luis Terrazas, procured fresh mounts, and were now apparently bound for the United States border. We cut across the angle and took the trail again, although the chase was now practically hopeless. Our only hope was to continue to push them on the possibility of giving them so little rest they might run into another command.

In three days we marched 125 miles, the last day in a hard rainstorm with the mules sinking fetlock deep into the soft ground. The scouts, their moccasins useless in the wet, were all barefoot, and several of them footsore. We had been forced to camp the day before at a water hole that contained alkali in the water. This weakened both men and mules. We were without food and several of the scouts were sick. We arrived at a hot spring on the edge of a cattle ranch owned by an English company whose local manager was Lord Delaval Beresford, a brother of Lord Charles Beresford.

As we were going into camp a force of Mexican soldiers following our trail came up with us. They were under the command of Colonel Mesilla, who informed me that two other Mexican forces, one of cavalry and one of infantry, had cut the trail ahead of us. Under our agreement with Mexico, when a Mexican force took the trail in advance of us we were required to abandon it and return to the United States, unless the Mexican commander desired to leave it to us. This Colonel Mesilla declined to do.

His decision was just as well, for we were practically at the end of our rope. Had the Colonel consented, I would have continued as far as possible for us to go, but it would undoubtedly have been at the cost of all of our stock and the risk of the lives of some of us. The trail was leading into a desert country bare of grass, with water only at great intervals and poor when found. We were again without food, having exhausted the three days' rations brought by Elliott. The men of Colonel Mesilla's command were but little better off than we in the matter of food. These Mexican soldiers were all convicts or ex-convicts, as was customary in those days. They were kept on the scantiest of rations—a little parched corn, dried beef, and sugar, with no more of these than absolutely necessary to carry them from one station to another. Nevertheless these poor souls, when they learned from the scouts that we were pretty hungry, insisted upon giving us a part of their scanty supply. Colonel Mesilla and his officers had ridden on.

The ground underfoot was ankle deep in mud, but near the spring was an adobe shed. Under the shed was water and mud, as everywhere else; but the roof was a peaked one, built in the American style, high at the ridge and sloping to the eaves. Two by three scantling tied the rafters at their base. We slept, or rather passed the night, on the scantling. Those of the scouts who could not find a roosting place on the scantling sat the night and rain out on the low adobe wall of the corral.

The nearest American point for us was El Paso, Texas, a hundred miles to the northeast but with a waterless, impassable desert intervening. Forty miles to the east was the Mexican Central station of San José. I decided to make for this place in hopes of getting food or transportation to El Paso. Then Dame Fortune decided to give us a breathing spell.

The next morning the rain had ceased and eight miles

to the east we saw a cluster of buildings, which the scouts said were the houses of the ranch owners and their store with lots of things to eat. Between us and the ranch houses was the bed of an ancient lake, dry most of the year but now filled by the rain. The Indians said the lake was not more than waist deep; to go around it meant a journey of fifteen or sixteen miles. We took the short cut through the water, at times up to our shoulder pits, but there was food ahead.

At the ranch we were met by Lord Delaval and his foreman, who were finally induced to stop laughing long enough to understand that we were as hungry as wolves. I had never met an Irishman who was a prohibitionist and Beresford proved no exception. We were, I think, on the third round while waiting for dinner to be served. Sieber, the three packers, and I began to feel uneasy. One and then another confessed to a prickly, burning sensation all over our skins from the shoulders down. Beresford had another good laugh.

"Go down to that hot spring in front of the house and jump into it," he said when he got his breath, "that lake you came through has alkali enough in it to take the hide off a rhinoceros." I never had the chance to try it on a rhino, but I can swear to the fact that it peeled us very effectively, notwithstanding our belated hot bath.

Beresford kindly furnished us supplies enough to reach the railroad station thirty miles east, where I expected to procure transportation for myself and men to El Paso, the packers to follow with the mules. I had not a cent in my pocket but would wire collect to the commanding officer at Fort Bliss.

The best laid plans of mice and men. The station agent would have no more to do with me than he would have had to do with Geronimo himself. Not for any pleading would he unbend. When I met him again, a few months later, he told me that he thought we were robbers mixed up with hostiles and that we were only waiting for the train to hold it up. He was on the point of wiring the train to stop until troops could be sent out, when he saw us moving off up the track in the direction of El Paso. Then he concluded that we were what we represented ourselves to be, but it was too late to do us any good.

We made El Paso, seventy-five miles in two days, afoot and on empty stomachs. Ten miles out of Juarez (then called Paso del Norte) I took the only mule left that could carry my weight faster than the Indians could walk, and went ahead to arrange with the Mexican military authorities for our crossing the bridge to El Paso. I knew there was a Mexican military force in Paso del Norte and after my reception by the station agent was not sure what their attitude might be.

When I rode up to the door of the commanding officer's office just after dark, I was certainly a sight for sore eyes. Ragged, dirty, a four months' beard, an old pair of black trousers that had been partially repaired with white thread blackened on the coffee pot, rawhide soles to my shoes, and my hair sticking through holes in my campaign hat; who would have accepted my statement that I was a commissioned officer of the United States army?

The Mexican colonel in command did not. He did not know that I understood Mexican and expressed himself freely, his adjutant acting as interpreter. The adjutant seemed to sense the fact that I was telling the truth and modified the Colonel's characterization of me as a thief, liar, bandit, and several other species of undesirable, winding up with the decision that he was going to put me in jail at once and jail my men as fast as they arrived in the town. If there were Indians among them, as I had asserted, they would be stood up before an adobe wall and shot.

Finally he asked me how I had got to Chihuahua, and I told him that I had crossed the Sierra Madre from Sonora, just north of the Rio Aros. That, he said, was positive proof that I was a liar as no one but Indians had ever crossed those mountains, the Mexican troops having tried many times without success. The mountains were impassable.

I was hungry and mad. Not half a mile away was El Paso. I lost my temper and gave the Colonel another piece of information. I told him that I had forty of the best fighters in the Apache nation, that they were by now near the outskirts of the town with double belts of cartridges, had had no food for two days, and knew that just across the river there was food in abundance. If he wanted to shoot any Apache he had better start now, as those Indians were going across unless he had men enough to stop them.

The old Colonel was evidently under the influence of liquor. Startled by this aspect of the situation, he came to his senses, wrote an order for our free passage of the bridge, and sent his adjutant with me. On the edge of town we met Sieber and the scouts. When the adjutant saw them he exclaimed:

"Valgame Dios!" (God bless me!)

Half an hour later, September 5, we were in Fort Bliss, our troubles at an end. In the twenty-four days since leaving the command we had marched over five hundred miles through a mountainous country in driving rains, much of the way in mud so deep that the mules sank above their fetlocks. Seldom were we able to ride. To avoid unexpectedly running into the hostiles, with the usual result of losing them, three scouts were kept constantly eight or ten miles in advance, they returning to us at night and being relieved by another three the next morning. Thus some of the ground was traversed three times.

At El Paso I met a friend of my father, a gentleman who was president of a New York company with large cattle and mining interests in northwestern Chihuahua, the heart of the Apache country in Mexico. His manager had just resigned and he persuaded me to leave the army and undertake the management of his properties. The headquarters of this enterprise was the Hacienda of Corralitos, 140 miles south of Deming, New Mexico. The Sierra Madre Mountains, where our troops were operating, formed the western boundary of his property. For many years the ranch had suffered from depredations of the Apache, who killed herders and cattle and stole horses. These raids were still to be expected as long as there were any Apache in northwestern Mexico. This alone would have continued my interest in the Geronimo campaign, but I had the added incentive of knowing that my friends were undergoing the dangers, hardships, and disappointments that I had left behind me.

In the following pages I will describe briefly, from official reports and first-hand information given me by those who took part in it, the finale of this remarkable campaign.

When Day's captives were sent to the border, Crawford sent a note to the General advising him that I was following the hostiles with only my scouts. When nothing was heard of me for a couple of weeks circumstantial reports that my scouts had mutinied and killed me were wired east. The New York papers published complimentary obituaries and gave the General the devil for risking so valuable a life. My mother, the daughter of an officer of the old army who had spent many years on Indian duty, took little stock in unconfirmed reports, but she cut out the obituaries and later sent them to me. Interesting reading!

At Bowie I submitted my resignation from the army to the General and requested leave of absence pending its acceptance. The General tried to dissuade me, but I had found the army unsuited to me and dreaded the return to routine duty when the Indian troubles were over.

Chapter XII

Crawford returns for reorganization. Fountain's command is ambushed. Crawford returns to Mexico. Surprises hostile camp. He is killed by Mexicans. Crook meets hostiles. Report of conference.

IN October, Crawford returned to the border to reorganize his command, the enlistment period of the scouts having expired.

On December 19, Lieutenant Fountain's command, pursuing a hostile band that had come up on a raid into Arizona, was ambushed. The surgeon, Doctor Maddox, and four men were killed and several wounded. The Indians suffered no loss as far as known.

About December 15, Crawford reëntered Mexico with a force composed only of scouts and pack trains. Lieutenant Maus had taken my place, with Lieutenant Shipp as assistant. Sieber started with the command, but was later recalled by the General, and Tom Horn, who had been taken along as Spanish interpreter, took his place as chief of scouts. Horn afterward wrote a book, or had one written for him, extolling his experiences among the Apache. This, however, was the first time he had anything to do in any official way with them, or was in the employ of the Government at all in connection with the management of Indians during my term of service—1882-85 inclusive. And other officers still living, who preceded me for several years on duty among these Indians, know nothing of his reputed connection with them during their time. I mention the matter only to refute some of the misleading trash that has been written and published of those times; most of it barefaced stealing of credit due some other fellow.

On the morning of January 11, 1886, Crawford surprised the hostile camp at a point on the Rio Aros about sixty or seventy miles above its junction with the Bavispe. He captured all their ponies and camp equipage, food, etc. Demoralized, Geronimo, Nachite, and Chihuahua opened negotiations for a surrender. The final agreement was to be entered into the next day and doubtless would have ended then and there all further resistance on their part, had not the Grim Reaper stepped in from an unexpected quarter.

A little after daylight on the morning of the twelfth a force of Mexican irregulars from the Sonora towns attacked Crawford's camp. Crawford ran forward, calling out that his command were friends and American soldiers. The firing stopped. The scouts had not returned the fire of the Mexicans. Maus, Shipp, and Horn were calling to both Mexicans and scouts to calm them. Crawford mounted a boulder to get better attention. Suddenly a single shot came from the Mexican force and Crawford fell with a bullet in his brain.

The firing then became general. Horn was wounded in the arm and one of the scouts seriously in the body. The scouts killed the Mexican commander, his second in command, and twelve or fifteen of his men, and wounded as many more before the firing could again be controlled. The hostiles in the meantime were interested spectators.

Crawford lingered five days, unconscious except for a brief three or four minutes just before his death, January 17, but he was unable to speak to Maus when the latter, his arms about him, tried to receive his last words. He was temporarily buried in Nacori, the nearest town to the scene of his death. Two months later his body was returned to the United States and interred at Kearney, Nebraska.

After the departure of the Mexicans, Maus resumed negotiations with the hostiles. They agreed to meet the General near the American border in "two moons" with a view to surrendering. On March 25, 1886, the meeting took place at Cañon de Los Embudos, Sonora, about twenty miles south of the American border and near the Chihuahua-Sonora line.

The result of this conference between General Crook and the hostiles is given in the following extracts from Senate Document No. 88, Fifty-first Congress, First session.

Camp El Cañon De Los Embudos,
20 Miles southeast of San Bernardino, Mex., March 26, 1886
(via Fort Bowie, Ariz., March 28, 1886)

Lieut. Gen. P. H. Sheridan,
Washington, D. C.

I met the hostiles yesterday at Lieutenant Maus's camp, they being located about 500 yards distant. I found them very independent, and as fierce as so many tigers; knowing what pitiless brutes they are themselves they mistrust every one else. After my talk with them it seemed as if it would be impossible to get any hold on them except on condition that they be allowed to return to the reservation on their old status. Today things look more favorable.

George Crook
Brigadier-General.

Confidential

Camp El Cañon De Los Embudos, Mexico,
March 27, 1886
(via Fort Bowie, Ariz., March 29, 1886)

Lieut. Gen. P. H. Sheridan, U.S.A.,
Washington, D. C.

In a conference with Geronimo and other Chiricahuas, I told them that they must decide at once upon unconditional surrender or fight it out; that in the latter event hostilities should be commenced at once and the last one of them killed, if it took fifty years. I told them to reflect on what they were to do before giving me their answer. The only propositions they would entertain were these three: that they should be sent east for not exceeding two years, taking with them such of the families as so desired, leaving at Apache, Nana, who is seventy years old and superannuated; or that they should all return to the reservation on their old status; or else return to the war path, with its attendant horrors. As I had to act at once, I have today accepted their surrender upon their first proposition.

Ka-e-te-na, the young chief, who less than two years ago was the worst Chiricahua of the whole lot, is now perfectly subdued. He is thoroughly reconstructed, has rendered me valuable assistance, and will be of great service in helping to control these Indians in the future. His stay at Alcatraz has worked a complete reformation in his character. I have not a doubt that similar treatment will produce [the] same results with the whole band, and by the end of that time the excitement will have died away. Mangus, with thirteen Chiricahuas, six of whom are bucks, is not with the other Chiricahuas. He separated from them in August last and has since held no communication with them. He has committed no depredations. As it would be likely to take at least a year to find him in the immense ranges of mountains to the south, I think it inadvisable to attempt any search at this time, especially as he will undoubtedly give himself up as soon as he hears what the others have done.

I start for Bowie tomorrow morning to reach there next night. I respectfully request to be informed whether or not my action has been approved and also that full instructions meet me at that point. The Chiricahuas start for Bowie tomorrow with the Apache scouts under Lieutenant Maus.

CONFERENCE

held March 25 and 27, 1886, at Cañon De Los Embudos (Cañon of the Funnels), 20 Miles S. SE. of San Bernardino Springs, Mexico, Between General Crook and the Hostile Chiricahua Chiefs.

First Day.

PRESENT: Geronimo, Catle, Chihuahua, Nachite, Captains Roberts and Bourke, Lieutenants Maus, Faison, and Shipp, Dr. Davis, Mr. Strauss, Mr. Moore, Mr. Daly, Mr. Fly, Ka-e-te-na, Alchisay, Charlie Roberts, Interpreters Concepcion, José Maria, Antonio Bresias, Mr. Montoya.

GENERAL CROOK. What have you to say; I have come all the way down from Bowie?

GERONIMO. I would like Concepcion to act as interpreter.

GENERAL CROOK. All right, but all the interpreters must remain to act as checks on each other.

GERONIMO. I want to talk first of the causes which led me to leave the reservation. I was living quietly and contented, doing and thinking of no harm, while at the Sierra Blanca. I don't know what harm I did to those three men, Chato, Mickey Free, and Lieutenant Davis. I was living peaceably and satisfied when people began to speak bad of me. I should be glad to know who started those stories. I was living peaceably with my family, having plenty to eat, sleeping well, taking care of my people, and perfectly contented. I don't know where those bad stories first came from. There we were doing well and my people well. I was behaving well. I hadn't killed a horse or man, American or Indian. I don't know what was the matter with the people in charge of us. They knew this to be so, and yet they said I was a bad man and the worst man there; but what harm had I done? I was living peaceably and well, but I did not leave on my own accord. Had I so left it would have been right to blame me; but as it is, blame those men who started this talk about me. Some time before I left an Indian named Wodiskay had a talk with me. He said, "they are going to arrest you," but I paid no attention to him, knowing that I had done no wrong; and the wife of Mangus, "Huera," told me that they were going to seize me and put me and Mangus in the guard-house, and I learned from the American and Apache soldiers, from Chato, and Mickey Free, that the Americans were going to arrest me and hang me, and so I left. I would like to know now who it was that gave the order to arrest me and hang me. I was living peaceably there with my family under the shade of the trees, doing just what General Crook had told me I must do and trying to follow his advice. I want to know now who it was ordered me to be arrested. I was praying to the light and to the darkness, to God and to the sun, to let me live quietly there with my family. I don't know what the reason was that people should speak badly of me. I don't want to be blamed. The fault was not mine. Blame those three men. With them is the fault, and find out who it was that began that bad talk about me.

I have several times asked for peace, but trouble has come from the agents and interpreters. I don't want what has passed to happen again. Now, I am going to tell you something else. The Earth-Mother is listening to me and I hope that all may be so arranged that from now on there shall be no trouble and that we shall always have peace. Whenever we see you coming to where we are, we think that it is God—you must come always with God. From this on I do not want that anything shall be told you about me even in joke. Whenever I have broken out, it has always been on account of bad talk. From this on I hope that people will tell me nothing but the truth. From this on I want to do what is right and nothing else and I do not want you to believe any bad papers about me. I want the papers sent you to tell the truth about me, because I want to do what is right. Very often there are stories put in the newspapers that I am to be hanged. I don't want that any more. When a man tries to do right, such stories ought not to be put in the newspapers. There are very few of my men left now. They have done some bad things but I want them all rubbed out now and let us never speak of them again. There are very few of us left. We think of our relations, brothers, brothers-in-law, father-in-law, etc., over on the reservation, and from this on we want to live at peace just as they are doing, and to behave as they are behaving. Sometimes a man does something and men are sent out to bring in his head. I don't want such things to happen to us. I don't want that we should be killing each other.

What is the matter that you don't speak to me? It would be better if you would speak to me and look with a pleasant face. It would make better feeling. I would be glad if you did. I'd be better satisfied if you would talk to me once in a while. Why don't you look at me and smile at me? I am the same man; I have the same feet, legs, and hands, and the sun looks down on me a complete man. I want you to look and smile at me.

General Crook. Let them finish their talk first.

Geronimo. I have not forgotten what you told me, although a long time has passed. I keep it in my memory. I am a complete man. Nothing has gone from my body. From here on I want to live at peace. Don't believe any bad talk you hear about me. The agents and the interpreter hear that somebody has done wrong, and they blame it all on me. Don't believe what they say. I don't want any of this bad talk in the future. I don't want those men who talked this way about me to be my agents any more. I want good men to be my agents and interpreters; people who will talk right. I want this peace to be legal and good. Whenever I meet you I talk good to you, and you to me, and peace is soon established; but when you go to the reservation you put agents and interpreters over us who do bad things. Perhaps they don't mind what you tell them, because I do not believe you would tell them to do bad things to us. In the future we don't want these bad men to be allowed near where we are to live. We don't want any more of that kind of bad talk. I don't want any man who will talk bad about me, and tell lies, to be there, because I am going to try and live well and peaceably. I want to have a good man put over me. While living I want to live well. I know I have to die sometime, but even if the heavens were to fall on me, I want to do what is right. I think I am a good man, but in the papers all over the world they say I am a bad man; but it is a bad thing to say so about me. I never do wrong without a cause. Every day I am thinking, how am I to talk to you to make you believe what I say; and, I think, too, that you are thinking of what you are to say to me. There is one God looking down on us all. We are all children of the one God. God is listening to me. The sun, the darkness, the winds, are all listening to what we now say.

To prove to you that I am telling you the truth, remember I sent you word that I would come from a place far away to speak to you here, and you see us now. Some have come on horseback and some on foot. If I were thinking bad, or if I had done bad, I would never have come here. If it had been my fault, would I have come so far to talk to you? I have told you all that has happened. I also had feared that I should never see Ka-e-te-na again, but here he is, and I want the past to be buried. I am glad to see Ka-e-te-na. I was afraid I should never see him again. That was one reason, too, why I left. I wish that Ka-e-te-na would be returned to us to live with his family. I now believe what I was told. Now I believe that all told me is true, because I see Ka-e-te-na again. I am glad to see him again, as I was told I should. We are all glad. My body feels good because I see Ka-e-te-na, and my breathing is good. Now I can eat well, drink well, sleep well, and be glad. I can go everywhere with good feeling. Now, what I want is peace in good faith. Both you and I think well and think alike. Well, we have talked enough and sat here long enough. I may have forgotten something, but if I remember it, I will tell you of it tonight, or tomorrow, or some other time. I have finished for today, but I'll have something more to say bye and bye.

General Crook. I have heard what you have said. It seems very strange that more than forty men should be afraid of three. If that was a fact, that you left the reservation for that reason, why did you kill innocent people, sneaking all over the country to do it. What did those innocent people do to you that you should kill them, steal their horses, and slip around in the rocks like coyotes?

Geronimo. We did not know what we had done to Davis, Mickey, Chato, and Wodiskay.

General Crook. But what has that to do with killing innocent people? There is not a week that you don't hear foolish stories in your own camp; but you are no child; you don't have to believe them. You promised me in the Sierra Madre that peace should last, but you have lied about [it]. All the Americans said that you were lying when I brought you up there to the reservation, and I have had a constant fight since with my own people to protect you from them. And the white people say that I am responsible for every one of those people who have been killed. When a man has lied to me once I want some better proof than his own word before I can believe him again. The feeling against having you come back to the reservation had about died out when you broke out again; but now it is worse than ever.

GERONIMO. That's why I want to ask who it was that ordered that I should be arrested.

GENERAL CROOK. That's all bosh. There were no orders for anyone to arrest you.

GERONIMO. Perhaps those who were going to arrest me were under somebody else's orders.

GENERAL CROOK. Geronimo, you sent up some of your people to kill Chato, and Lieutenant Davis, and then you started the story that they had killed them, and thus you got a great many of your people to go out.

GERONIMO. That's not so. You'll know one of these days that it's not so.

GENERAL CROOK. Everything you did on the reservation is known. There is no use for you to try and talk nonsense. I am no child. You must make up your own mind whether you will stay out on the warpath or surrender unconditionally. If you stay out, I'll keep after you and kill the last one, if it takes fifty years. You are making a great fuss about seeing Ka-e-te-na. Over a year ago I asked you if you wanted me to bring Ka-e-te-na back but you said no. It is a good thing for Geronimo that we did not bring Ka-e-te-na back, because Ka-e-te-na has now more sense than all the rest of the Chiricahua put together.

GERONIMO. I am a man of my word. I am telling the truth, and why I left the reservation.

GENERAL CROOK. You told me the same thing in the Sierra Madre, but you lied.

GERONIMO. Then how do you want me to talk to you? I have but one mouth; I can't talk with my ears.

GENERAL CROOK. Your mouth talks too many ways.

GERONIMO. If you think I am not telling the truth, then I don't think you came down here in good faith.

GENERAL CROOK. I come with the same faith as when I went down to the Sierra Madre. You told me the same things there that you are telling me now: What evidence have I of your sincerity? How do I know whether or not you are lying to me? Have I ever lied to you?

GERONIMO. I was living at peace with my family on the reservation. Why were those stories started about me?

GENERAL CROOK. How do I know? Are not stories started in your own camp every day?

GERONIMO. There is no other captain so great as you. I thought you ought to know about those stories, and who started them.

GENERAL CROOK. Who were all the Indians that those stories were started about?

GERONIMO. If they talked only of me I should not have minded, but all the Indians know that the stories were about them too. If you don't want to believe me I can prove it by all the men, women and children of the White Mountain Apache.

GENERAL CROOK. Answer my question.

GERONIMO. They wanted to seize me and Mangus.

GENERAL CROOK. Then why did Natchez and Chihuahua go out?

GERONIMO. Because they were afraid the same thing would happen to them.

GENERAL CROOK. Who made them afraid?

GERONIMO. All the Indians here with me saw the troops and scouts getting ready to go out to arrest us. That is the reason they went out.

GENERAL CROOK. But what did you tell those Indians?

GERONIMO. The only thing I told them was that I heard I was going to be seized and killed, that's all.

GENERAL CROOK. But why did you send up some of your people to kill Lieutenant Davis and Chato?

GERONIMO. I did not tell them to do anything of the kind. If I had said anything like that these Indians would say so.

GENERAL CROOK. That's just what they do say; and you reported that they were killed and that is the reason so many went out with you.

GERONIMO. If that is so, here are a number of White Mountain Indians. They ought to know whether that was so or not.

GENERAL CROOK. But they all know it up there.

GERONIMO. Well, here is a White Mountain sergeant, a man like that won't lie; ask him.

GENERAL CROOK. Plenty of your own friends up there at Fort Apache say it is so.

GERONIMO. This man ought to know something about it; ask him.

GENERAL CROOK. Very likely he don't know anything about it. Those we asked up there *did* know.

GERONIMO. Whenever I wanted to talk with Lieutenant Davis, I spoke by day or by night. I never went to him in a hidden manner. Maybe some of these men know about it. Perhaps you had better ask them.

GENERAL CROOK. I have said all I have to say. You had better think it over tonight and let me know in the morning.

GERONIMO. All right, we'll talk tomorrow; I may want to ask you some questions, too, as you have asked me some.

Second Day (*March 27*).

PRESENT. Same as on first day.

CHIHUAHUA. I am very glad to see you and have this talk with you. It is as you say, we are always in danger out here. I hope from this time on we may live better with our families and not do any harm to anybody. I am anxious to behave. I think the sun is looking down upon me and the earth is listening. I am thinking better. It seems to me that I have seen the One who makes the rain and sends the winds; or He must have sent you to this place. I surrender myself to you because I believe in you and you do not deceive us. You must be our God. I am satisfied with all that you do. You must be the one who makes the green pastures, who sends the rain, who commands the winds. You must be the one who sends the fresh fruits that appear on the trees every year. There are many men in the world who are big chiefs and command many people, but you, I think, are the greatest of them all, or you wouldn't come out here to see us. I want you to be a father to me and treat me as your son. I want you to have pity on me. There is no doubt that all you do is right, because all you do is just the same as if God did it. Everything you do is right. So I consider, so I believe you to be. I trust in all you say; you do not deceive. All the things you tell us are facts. I am now in your hands. I place myself at your disposition. I surrender myself to you. Do with me as you please. I shake your hand [shaking hands]. I want to come right into your camp with my family and stay with you. I don't want to stay away at a distance. I want to be right where you are. I have roamed these mountains from water to water. Never have I found the place where I could see my father or my mother, until today I see you my father. I surrender to you now and I don't want any more bad feelings or bad talk. I am going over to stay with you in your camp. Whenever a man raises anything, even a dog, he thinks well of it and tries to raise it right and treat it well. So I want you to feel toward me and be good to me and don't let people say bad things about me. Now I surrender to you and go with you. When we are traveling together on the road or anywhere else, I hope you'll talk to me once in a while. I think a great deal of Alchisay and Ka-e-te-na and they think a great deal of me, and I hope some day to be all the same as their brother. [Shakes hands again with General Crook.] How long will it be before I can stay with these friends?

General Crook. After a while. [Chihuahua shakes hands again.]

Chihuahua. If you don't let me go back to the reservation, I would like you to send my family with me wherever you send me. I have a daughter at Camp Apache, and some others, relations of myself and of my band at San Carlos.

Wherever you want to send me I wish you would also send them.

GENERAL CROOK. But will they want to go with you?

CHIHUAHUA. If they want to come, let them come; if they want to stay there, let them. [Shakes hands.] I ask you to find out if they are willing to go or not.

NACHEZ. What Chihuahua says I say. I surrender just the same as he did. I surrender to you just the same as he did. What he has said I say. I give you my word, I give you my body. I surrender; I have nothing more to say than that. When I was free I gave orders, but now I surrender to you. I throw myself at your feet. You now order and I obey. What you tell me to do I do. [Shakes hands.] Now that I have surrendered I am glad. I'll not have to hide behind rocks and mountains; I'll go across the open plain. I'll now sleep well, eat contentedly, and be satisfied, and so will my people. There may be lots of men who have bad feelings against us. I will go wherever you may see fit to send us, where no bad talk will be spoken of us. When I was out in the mountains I thought I should never see you again, but I am glad because I now see you and have a talk with you. I think now it is best for us to surrender and not remain out in the mountains like fools, as we have been doing. I have nothing further to say. I surrender to you, and hope you will be kind to us, as you have always been a good friend to the Indians and tried to do what was right for them. I have changed all my thoughts. I surrender to you. Whatever you do to me is right, and all these men here are witnesses that I surrender to you. The day has at last come when I could see you, talk to and surrender to you. I have always believed all you told me. You don't lie to me. I hope from this on you will see that I am in earnest, and will believe what I say. This is not the first time I've talked with you, and I hope it won't be the last. I surrender to you, and place myself in your hands. I'll do what you say, but I want you from time to time to talk with me. I think a great deal of Alchisay and Ka-e-te-na and I know you do too. I hope they will think as much of me as you do of them. I don't know where you are going to send me, but I am afraid I will not see Alchisay or Ka-e-te-na again.

GENERAL CROOK. Don't worry about that.

CHIHUAHUA. That's all I have to say. I have spoken with all my heart. [Shakes hands with General Crook.] When shall we start from here?

GENERAL CROOK. I am going back to Bowie tomorrow, as I have much work to do there. Alchisay, Ka-e-te-na, and the scouts will stay with you and take you over to Bowie. I think you will start in the morning. There are no rations here. Every day I will have a courier from Lieutenant Maus to tell me where you are and how you are doing.

CHIHUAHUA. Our stock is very poor, and I was afraid that I'd have to travel too fast.

GENERAL CROOK. Not at all; you will come along in good time.

CHIHUAHUA. I will send you word each day.

GENERAL CROOK. All right. Ka-e-te-na can write your letters for you. [Chihuahua shakes hands with General Crook.]

GERONIMO. Two or three words are enough. I have little to say. I surrender myself to you. [Shakes hands with General Crook.] We are all comrades, all one family, all one band. What the others say I say also. I give myself up to you. Do with me what you please. I surrender. Once I moved about like the wind. Now I surrender to you and that is all. [Shakes hands with General Crook.] I don't want any one to say any wrong thing about me any way. I surrender to you and want to be just as if I were in your pocket. My heart is yours, and I hope yours will be mine. [Shakes hands.] Now I feel like your brother, and Ka-e-te-na is my brother also [Shakes hands.] I was very far from here. Almost nobody could go to that place. But I sent you word I wanted to come in here, and here I am. I have no lies in my heart. Whatever you tell me is true. We are all satisfied of that. I hope the day may come when my word shall be as strong with you as yours is with me. That's all I have to say now, except a few words. I should like to have my wife and daughter come to meet me at Fort Bowie or Silver Creek.

General Crook. They can meet you on the road somewhere. I can't tell where. You must not pay any attention to the talk you hear. There are some people who can no more control their talk than the wind can.

Geronimo. I want now to let Alchisay and Ka-e-te-na to speak a few words. They have come a long ways and I want to hear them speak.

Ka-e-te-na. Let Alchisay speak for me. I have a sore throat.

Alchisay. They have all surrendered. There is nothing more to be done, but I'll speak only a few words. I am mad with Captain Bourke because he is writing down what I say. I am not a captain but a small man, and what I say don't count.

General Crook. It's best to put everything on paper. When you are dead your children and your children's children can know what you have said. It is not this kind of paper that lies; it's the newspapers.

Alchisay. I am talking now for these Chiricahua. They have surrendered. I don't want you to have any bad feelings toward them. They are all good friends now and I am glad they have surrendered, because they are all the same people—all one family with me; just like when you kill a deer, all its parts are of the one body; so with these Chiricahua. Now they have surrendered, they are one body with the rest of the Apache. You are our chief; the only one we have; there is no other. No matter where you send these Chiricahua we hope to hear that you have treated them kindly. All these lies in the newspapers, don't mind them; if you are satisfied with us we don't care what the newspapers say. A hen has many chickens; she goes ahead, the chickens follow; so you are going over to Apache Pass and we are coming along behind you. Now, we want to travel along the open road and drink the waters of the Americans, and not hide in the mountains; we want to live without danger or discomfort. I am very glad that the Chiricahua surrendered, and that I have been able to talk for them. After I get back to Camp Apache I want to talk a little for myself. We want you to be in charge of us and no one else; you know me well; I have never told you a lie, nor have you ever told me a lie, and now I tell you that these Chiricahua really want to do what is right and live at peace. If they don't, then I lie, and you must not believe me any more. It's all right; you are going ahead to Fort Bowie; I want you to carry away in your pocket all that has been said here today.

General Crook. You mean all that all the Chiricahua have said.

Alchisay. That's what I mean.

Chapter XIII

Geronimo again proves faithless. Crook asks to be relieved. Miles in command. Mexican citizens kill three hostiles. Miles' policy. Lebo's fight. Hatfield's command ambushed. Lawton's operations. Miles learns that some of the hostiles are weary of warfare. Sends for Gatewood. Gatewood enters Geronimo's camp and induces him to surrender to Miles.

THE night after the General left, following his conference with the hostiles, an American named Tribolet, who had a small camp near San Bernardino Springs on the border, began selling mescal to both scouts and hostiles. Maus sent Shipp to destroy such liquor as he could find, but the damage had been done. Geronimo, Nachite, and a dozen or more of the hostiles got drunk and that night twenty men, thirteen women, three boys, and three girls under the leadership of Geronimo and Nachite slipped away from the camp and went back to Mexico. Two days later, however, two of the warriors deserted them, rejoined Chihuahua's party, and went on to Bowie.

The escape of Geronimo's party gave rise to the following telegraphic correspondence between Sheridan and Crook, resulting in Crook being relieved at his own request and Miles being assigned to command of the Department.

Headquarters Department of Arizona.
In the field, Fort Bowie, Ariz., March 30, 1886.

Lieut. Gen. P. H. SHERIDAN,
Washington, D. C.:

A courier just in from Lieutenant Maus reports that during last night Geronimo and Natchez with twenty men and thirteen women, left his camp taking no stock. He states that there was no apparent cause for their leaving. Two dispatches received from him this morning reported everything going on well and the Chiricahua in good spirits. Chihuahua and twelve men remained behind. Lieutenant Maus, with his scouts, except enough to take the other prisoners to Bowie, have gone in pursuit.

GEORGE CROOK,
Brigadier-General.

Headquarters Army of the United States,
Washington, D. C., March 31, 1886

General GEORGE CROOK,
Fort Bowie, Ariz.:

Your dispatch of yesterday received. It has occasioned great disappointment. It seems strange that Geronimo and party could have escaped without the knowledge of the scouts.

P. H. SHERIDAN,
Lieutenant-General.

Headquarters Department of Arizona,
In the Field, Fort Bowie, Ariz., March 31, 1886

Lieut. Gen. P. H. SHERIDAN,
Washington, D. C.:

Your dispatch of 31st received. There can be no question that the scouts were thoroughly loyal, and would have prevented the hostiles leaving had it been possible. When they left their camp with our scouts they scattered over the country so as to make surprise impossible, and they located their camp with this in view, nor would they all remain in camp at one time. They kept more or less full of mescal. They had so tamed down since we first met them that some of the most prominent were hunting their ponies unarmed the evening of the night they left.

George Crook,
Brigadier-General.

Headquarters Department of Arizona,
In the Field, Fort Bowie, Ariz., March 31, 1886

Lieut. Gen. P. H. Sheridan,
Washington, D. C.:

In reply to your dispatch of March 30, to enable you to clearly understand [the] situation, it should be remembered that the hostiles had an agreement with Lieutenant Maus, that they were to be met by me twenty-five miles below the line; that no regular troops were to be present. While I was very averse to such an agreement I had to abide by it, as it already had been entered into. We found them in camp on a rocky hill about 500 yards from Lieutenant Maus in such a position that a thousand men could not have surrounded them with any possibility of capturing them. They were able upon the approach of an enemy being signaled to scatter and escape through dozens of ravines and cañons, which would shelter them from pursuit until they reached the higher ranges in the vicinity. They were armed to the teeth, having the most improved guns and all the ammunition they could carry. The clothing and other supplies lost in the fight with Crawford had been replaced by new blankets and shirts obtained in Mexico. Lieutenant Maus with [the] Apache scouts was camped at the nearest point the hostiles would agree to his approaching. Even had I been disposed to betray the confidence they placed in me, it would have been simply an impossibility to get white troops to that point either by day or by night without their knowledge, and had I attempted to do this the whole band would have stampeded back to the mountains. So suspicious were they that never more than from five to eight of the men came into our camp at one time, and to have attempted the arrest of those would have stampeded the others to the mountains. Even after the march to Bowie began we were compelled to allow them to scatter. They would not march in a body, and had any efforts been made to keep them together they would have broken for the mountains. My only hope was to get their confidence on the march through Ka-e-a-tena and other confidential Indians, and finally put them on the cars; and until this was done it was impossible even to disarm them.

George Crook,
Brigadier-General, Commanding.

Washington, D. C. April 1, 1886
(Received 2.11 P. M.)

General George Crook,
Fort Bowie, Ariz.:

Your dispatch of March 31, received. I do not see what you can now do except to concentrate your troops at the best points and give protection to the people. Geronimo will undoubtedly enter upon other raids of murder and robbery, and as the offensive campaign against him with scouts has failed, would it not be best to take up defensive and give protection to the people and business interests of Arizona and New Mexico? The infantry might be stationed by companies on certain points requiring protection, and the cavalry patrol between them. You have in your department forty-six companies of infantry and forty companies of cavalry, and ought to be able to do a good deal with such a force. Please send me a statement of what you contemplate for the future.

P. H. Sheridan,
Lieutenant-General.

Headquarters Department of Arizona,
In the Field, Fort Bowie, Ariz., April 1, 1886

Lieut. Gen. P. H. SHERIDAN,
Washington, D. C.:

Your dispatch of today received. It has been my aim throughout present operations to afford the greatest amount of protection to life and property interests, and troops have been stationed accordingly. Troops can not protect beyond a radius of one-half mile from their camp. If offensive movements against the Indians are not resumed they may remain quietly in the mountains for an indefinite time without crossing the line, and yet their very presence there will be a constant menace, and require the troops in this department to be at all times in position to repel sudden raids; and so long as any remain out they will form a nucleus for disaffected Indians from the different agencies in Arizona and New Mexico to join. That the operations of the scouts in Mexico have not proved as successful as was hoped is due to the enormous difficulties that they have been compelled to encounter, from the nature of the Indians they have been hunting, and the character of the country in which they have operated, and of which persons not thoroughly conversant with both can have no conception. I believe that the plan upon which I have conducted operations is the one most likely to prove successful in the end. It may be, however, that I am too much wedded to my own views in this matter, and as I have spent nearly eight years of the hardest work of my life in this department, I respectfully request that I may be now relieved from its command. [See G. O. No. 15, series 1886, relieving General Crook from Command.]

GEORGE CROOK,
Brigadier-General.

Geronimo, Nachite, and those with them went south to the vicinity of the Mexican town of Casas Grandes in northwestern Chihuahua, forty miles south of my mining and cattle headquarters at Corralitos. From their camp in the mountains they sent three of their party into the town to see if they could patch up one of their periodical peaces with the Casas Grandes Mexicans. It was in this town that Juh had become drunk and was drowned in the river a few miles above the town.

The Mexicans, knowing that American troops were after Geronimo and hot on his trail, had no fear of reprisals. They received his ambassadors of good will with éclat, got them drunk, disarmed them, stood them up before an adobe wall, and made "good Injin" of them; then they sent a courier to me at Corralitos to apprise me of the good news.

Of the forty-three men and one hundred and one women and children who left the Reservation May 17, 1885, there were left now, when Miles relieved Crook, but seventeen men, including Geronimo and Nachite, with nineteen women and children.

Crook was convinced that the only way to complete the subjugation of this small remnant was relentless pursuit with the scouts until they were all killed, or so weary of being chased from pillar to post they would be disposed to surrender on terms Crook felt he could expect to exact of them. We have seen that Sheridan disagreed with this plan and Crook was relieved, Miles taking his place April 12.

In his book, *Personal Recollections and Observations of General Nelson A. Miles* (Chicago, 1896), Miles gives one hundred pages, about one-sixth of the entire book, to his efforts to accomplish the subjugation of this remnant of the hostiles with five thousand troops at his command. He must have considered it a feat of no small importance. I will sketch it briefly.

Miles adopted a policy midway between Crook's and that demanded of Crook by Sheridan. He garrisoned all water holes and ranches he thought might be subject to attack and established twenty-five or thirty signal points on prominent mountain peaks, using the heliostat for signaling. The scouts were dismissed, except a few to be used for trailers with the various cavalry and infantry commands who were to pursue the hostiles.

A principal pursuit column was organized under Captain H. W. Lawton, Fourth Cavalry. The command as at first organized was composed of infantry, mounted cavalry, and about a dozen Indian trailers, and had orders to operate only south of the American border. Five days in the mountains of northern Sonora finished the mounted cavalry. They were dismounted, the horses were discarded, and the men joined the infantry.

While these preparations were going on the hostiles were not idle. During the last days of April a party of them came up from Mexico, raided over a large part of central and southern Arizona, pursued constantly by various commands in futile efforts to destroy or capture them, and finally escaped back into Sonora after killing near a score of people with no loss to themselves.

On May 5, Captain Lebo overtook and fought them in the Pinito Mountains of northern Sonora with a loss of one of his men killed and one wounded. No damage was done to the hostiles so far as known.

Ten days later, on May 15, Hatfield's troop struck them in a small mountain range between the Santa Cruz and San Pedro rivers, and captured their ponies and camp equipage. As Hatfield was making his way out of the mountains through an unknown country, back to water for his men and stock, the Indians ambushed his scattered command in a box cañon, killed his blacksmith and cook, wounded the first and second sergeants, and recovered their ponies. So far as known they suffered no loss themselves.

Two days following Hatfield's fight the same band raided north again as far as the White Mountain Reservation, where one of them deserted and went in among the Chiricahua and Warm Springs, who had not taken part in the outbreak. This man, Ki-e-ta, was later selected as one of the two Chiricahua to accompany Gatewood to Mexico in his successful effort to induce Geronimo and Nachite to surrender to Miles.

Meantime, Lawton's command was operating in the mountains of Sonora. In his official report to Miles he states:

> Numbers of other commands were in the field and the hostiles were frequently met and pursued by them. During this portion of the campaign, (to July 5) my command marched, including side scouts and reconnaissances, 1,396 miles, nearly all of which distance was over rough, high mountains.

To this I may add that many of these mountains rose eight or ten thousand feet above the adjacent Sonora valleys. In one instance we, Crawford's command, were thirty hours gaining the summit of a range after leaving the neighboring river bottom. During those two days we lost over a dozen animals that fell and rolled down the slope, killing themselves against rocks or trees.

Lawton's operations continued until the surrender of the hostiles on September 5. The net, tangible result of these four months of strenuous effort was the capture, on July 14, by Indian scouts under Lieutenant Brown, of the ponies and camp equipage of one party of hostiles.

No other element of Lawton's force was engaged in this capture. Lawton with his infantry and dismounted cavalry did not reach the hostile camp until the Indians had disappeared, leaving Brown and his Apache scouts in possession.

Being deprived of their ponies and scant camp equipage meant little to the hostiles. Seven times in fifteen months this happened to them, and seven times within a week or ten days they reëquipped themselves through raids on Mexican settlements or American ranches.

Following Brown's capture of this camp, Lawton reports:

> Their trail was again discovered and followed up the Aros River, thence northwest until the twenty-third of July. My supplies were nearly exhausted and the heavy rains threatened a rise of the Aros River in my rear, so I moved back across the stream to meet the fresh supplies which were on the way from the supply camp under escort of the cavalry. During this short campaign the suffering was intense. The country was indescribably rough and the weather swelteringly hot, with heavy rains day and night. The endurance of the men was tried to the utmost limit. Disabilities resulting from excessive fatigue reduced the infantry to fourteen men, and they were worn out and without shoes.

Crawford's command had operated in this same country for four months of the previous year under identically the same conditions as to heat and rain; and we found that to wear the hostiles down with regular troops was impossible. Without Apache scouts they could not follow the trails; nor had they the endurance to keep up with the scouts in these mountains where the scouts had been born and bred. They were only a hindrance to rapid movement where rapid movement was essential to success. As well match Londoners against the Alpine Swiss.

Conditions were very different from what they had been when our troops fought these Indians ten and twelve years before, or even in Victorio's time, 1880-81. Then the hostiles were in greater number and led by bolder chiefs, who frequently stopped to fight us if they had anything better than an even break. It was now no longer a question of fighting them but purely one of wearing them down.

While at Fort Apache, July 1, to inspect the condition of the Chiricahua and Warm Spring bands who had refused to leave with Geronimo and Mangus, Miles learned from the Chiricahua, Ki-e-ta, who had deserted on the hostile raid in May, that some of the followers of Geronimo and Nachite were, like himself, tired of warfare, and that the entire band might be persuaded to listen to reason and agree to surrender if two or three men they knew were sent to talk to them. Ki-e-ta consented to be one of the emissaries, and an influential Chiricahua known as Martine was selected as the second member of the ambassadorial party.

But it was essential that some officer with authority should be the bearer of Miles's tender of terms; and this officer must be one known to Geronimo, and who knew him, if anything tangible was to result. Any strange officer attempting to enter Geronimo's camp would be shot on sight.

Crawford was dead. I had resigned and would doubtless not have been selected for the duty even had I remained in the service. Gatewood had been relieved from duty at Fort Apache the previous December, and had rejoined his regiment at Fort Stanton, New Mexico.

He had met Geronimo and other chiefs occasionally during the winter we were in camp near Fort Apache. What was of more importance, Geronimo knew the high esteem in which Gatewood was held by the White Mountain Apache, who had been under his care for more than three years. Miles sent for Gatewood.

Cool, quiet, courageous; firm when convinced of right, but intolerant of wrong; with a thorough knowledge of Apache character and conversant with the causes leading to the outbreak, he was the ideal selection for as difficult and, personally, dangerous assignment as ever fell to the lot of an officer of our army in dealing with the aborigines.

Through the courtesy of his son, Major Charles B. Gatewood, U.S. Army, Retired, to whom I am indebted, also, for other data of events following my resignation, I am able to give from his father's personal memoirs a brief account of his experiences as bearer of the flag of truce.

In giving Gatewood his assignment, Miles instructed him to get an escort of twenty-five men at Fort Bowie, warning him not to go near the hostiles without this escort for fear of being captured and held for ransom. In this Miles showed his lack of understanding of the Apache. Not even five, to say nothing of twenty-five, soldiers could have come within rifle range of the hostile camp without being fired on.

The commanding officer at Bowie was loath to furnish the escort but promised that it would be furnished by the commanding officer at Cloverdale, on the border. There Gatewood found only part of a company of infantry and no animals on which to mount them. Similar commands encountered on his way south were in just as bad shape and Gatewood continued on to Lawton's command on the Aros River, two hundred miles south of the border, with his small party organized at Bowie. This party consisted of the two Indians, Ki-e-ta and Martine; George Wratten, interpreter; Frank Houston, packer; and a man known as "Old Tex" Whaley, courier.

Soon after crossing the border he met a troop of the Fourth Cavalry under command of Lieutenant James Parker, with infantry detachments under Lieutenants Bullard and Richardson, who accompanied him to Lawton's camp, then returned north.

Lawton knew nothing of the whereabouts of the hostiles, and Gatewood remained with him until about the fifteenth of August; then word was received that Geronimo's party was near Fronteras, a Mexican town of northern Sonora. With an escort of six men given him by Lawton, Gatewood and his party arrived at Fronteras to learn from Lieutenant Wilder, who was in camp there with a small detachment of troops, that two of the hostile women had been in the town a few days previously to obtain supplies and sound the Mexican authorities on the question of a treaty of peace.

From Wilder, Gatewood got Tom Horn and José Maria as additional interpreters and six men to replace the men he was constantly sending back as couriers to Lawton, some twenty-five miles away, with reports of his progress.

Taking the trail of the women six miles east of Fronteras, Gatewood and his party followed it for three days, a piece of flour sack on a stick being held aloft as a flag of truce. As he was going into camp on the Bavispe River about sundown of the third day, Martine, who with Ki-e-ta had been in advance, returned to him with the information that the hostiles were in camp about four miles away on a lofty peak of the Torres Mountains in the bend of the Bavispe, where it makes its turn from north to south near the northern border of Sonora.

Both of the Indians had been in Geronimo's camp, and had informed him of their mission. Geronimo had detained Ki-e-ta and sent Martine back with the message that he would talk to Gatewood only. That night Lieutenant Brown with the thirty scouts from Lawton's command arrived in Gatewood's camp; but when they started forward with him the next morning they were met by three armed Chiricahua who told them they must return to their camp and remain there, as must any other scouts or troops who came. That only Gatewood and his small party would be permitted any nearer the place designated for the conference. This was a little glade on the bank of the Bavispe about two miles from Gatewood's camp.

Gatewood thus describes the meeting:

By squads the hostiles came in, unsaddled and turned out their ponies to graze. Among the last to arrive was Geronimo. He laid his rifle down twenty feet away and came and shook hands, remarking my apparent bad health and asking what was the matter. The tobacco having been passed around, of which I had brought fifteen pounds on my saddle, he took a seat alongside as near as he could get, the others in a semi-circle, and announced that the whole party was there to listen to General Miles' message.

It took but a minute to say "Surrender, and you will be sent with your families to Florida, there to await the decision of the

President as to your final disposition. Accept these terms or fight it out to the bitter end."

A silence of weeks seemed to fall on the party. They sat there with never a movement, regarding me intently. Finally Geronimo passed a hand across his eyes, made his hands tremble, and asked me for a drink.

Geronimo was greatly disappointed when he found that Gatewood had no liquor with him and explained that the hostiles had been on a drunk for three days with mescal purchased from the Mexicans of Fronteras. The mescal gone, they were all a little shaky, and had hoped that Gatewood had also laid in a supply at Fronteras.

Geronimo's first reaction to Miles's demands was an emphatic refusal. He and his people would leave the warpath only on condition that they be allowed to return to the Reservation, reoccupy their farms, be furnished with the usual rations, clothing, and farming implements, and be guaranteed immunity from punishment. The discussion continued all day, neither party gaining a point.

"Take us to the Reservation or fight," says Gatewood, "was his ultimatum as he looked me in the eye."

Gatewood returned to his camp with an agreement to meet the hostiles again the next morning and continue the argument. As he was about to leave, he had the opportunity to tell Nachite, who had inquired about his mother and daughter, who had gone in with Chihuahua's party six months before, that they with all of Chihuahua's party had been sent to Florida and that all the Chiricahua and Warm Springs at Fort Apache were being sent there. I will have something to say of this in conclusion.

When Gatewood returned to the council he found the

hostiles more inclined to listen to his arguments. Nachite was anxious about his family and leaned now to Gatewood's side. Geronimo, seeing that he was losing ground, began to inquire what kind of a man Miles was, having never known anything of him. Gatewood described Miles in glowing terms; but fear and suspicion on the part of the Indians prolonged the discussion till near sunset. Gatewood was preparing to return to his camp, where Lawton had arrived that day, when Geronimo suddenly said to him:

"We want your advice. Consider yourself not a white man but one of us. Remember all that has been said today and tell us what we should do."

Gatewood replied: "Trust General Miles and surrender to him."

The next morning the pickets passed a call for "Bay-chen-day-sen"—Long Nose—Gatewood's name among the Apache.

Gatewood met Geronimo, Nachite, and several more of the hostiles half a mile from his camp. They told him that they had decided to take his advice, go to the border, and surrender to Miles. But knowing the intense feeling against them and that other commands than Lawton's, both Mexican and American, were in the field and might be encountered *en route* to the border, they made the following stipulations: that they were not to surrender their arms until after their talk with Miles; that Lawton's command should march near them to protect them from other commands that might be encountered; that Gatewood should march with them and sleep in their camp. Gatewood agreed to these stipulations, and Geronimo and Nachite then went with him to Lawton's camp, where the arrangement was explained to Lawton and approved by him.

The following is a true copy of a note in the possession of Major Gatewood, through whose courtesy I am able to make it public for the first time.

Lt. Gatewood, U.S.A.
Care Geronimo,
Sonora,
Mex.

My Dear Gatewood:

I have just arrived in Brown's camp and have rec'd your notes. My Pack Train got off the trail yesterday, and will not be in until in the night. I have sent Lt. Smith back on fresh horse to bring up your tobacco and some rations and will send them over to you as soon as they arrive. I have ordered them to come forward if it kills the mules. It will be too late for me to go over tonight, and besides I do not wish to interfere with you, but will come over if you wish me. Send a man back to conduct pack mules over, and write me what you want. I *hope* and *trust* your efforts will meet with success.

Yours,
(Signed) H. W. Lawton, Capt.

Aug. 24, '86
A true copy:
C. B. Gatewood
Major, U.S.A., Ret.

As Miles never saw Geronimo until he met him with Gatewood at the border, September 3, 1886, this note of Lawton's should settle the controversy over who "captured Geronimo." At the time the note was written Lawton was in camp where Gatewood had camped when he first got in touch with the hostiles and was overtaken by Brown. The Indians had turned Brown's scouts back and specified that no troops or scouts should approach nearer than that point while they were negotiating with Gatewood, four miles away. That was as near as Lawton got to them until after they had agreed with Gatewood on the terms of their surrender.

If further proof of the respective parts of Lawton and Gatewood in the surrender of Geronimo were needed, it is furnished by General Parker whose account of the campaign I will again refer to in closing my story.

General Parker was ordered to furnish Gatewood an escort and accompanied him until they met Lawton on the Aros River. General Parker thus describes the meeting:

> When told about Gatewood, Lawton objected strongly to taking him with his command. "I get my orders from President Cleveland direct," he said. "I am ordered to hunt Geronimo down and kill him. I can not treat with him." . . .
>
> I stayed three days with Lawton. Before I left him he agreed to take with him Gatewood and his Indians. "But," said he, "if I find Geronimo I will attack him—I refuse to have anything to do with this plan to treat with him—if Gatewood wants to treat with him he can do it on his own hook."

Credit is due Lawton for four months of strenuous work under mighty discouraging conditions. Lawton himself never claimed more. And what of the scout commands of Crawford and Wirt Davis, who operated for eleven and eight months, respectively, under the same conditions, in the same terrain; killed the only hostiles killed by our forces; captured thirty of their women and children in combat, and forced the surrender of Chihuahua's band of fourteen men, two half-grown boys and fifty-seven women and children in all, two-thirds of all the hostiles who left the Reservation in May, 1885—leaving but nineteen men and twenty-eight women and children for Lawton's and other commands to contend with. And of these, six refused to surrender to Miles and were later accounted for by Kosterlitzky's Gendarmerie.

Lawton was luckily in at the death; but we should not forget those others who also "rode to the hounds."

Chapter XIV

Capture of Mangus. All the Chiricahua and Warm Springs are arrested at Fort Apache and sent to Florida. Banquet to Miles and Lawton. Gatewood's reward. Bourke's comment. General Parker's comment.

ON their way up to Fort Bowie after the agreement to surrender, two of the hostiles repented of their action and deserted at night, fleeing to Mexico with two women, a girl, and a boy. Colonel Kosterlitzky, commanding the Gendarmerie (Mexican border guards for the states of Chihuahua and Sonora), advised me from time to time of their being surprised and killed, one or two at a time, till only one woman was left, who, presumably, made her way back to the Reservation.

Mangus with two men, three women, two half-grown boys, a girl, and four small children were still in Mexico. In his *Personal Recollections,* Miles states (pp. 529-530):

> After the surrender of Geronimo and Natchez, a small band of hostiles under a chief named Mangus, who had not been with the other hostiles, still remained out, and to secure them I organized a force under Lieutenant C. B. Johnson, who followed them down through parts of old Mexico and back up into and through New Mexico.

The General's memory has played him false. Johnson saw no sign of Mangus, and trailed him nowhere, in Mexico. No one knew of Mangus' whereabouts until early in October, 1886. Moreover, in the General's further statement that "On the 14th of October, the Indians having been reported in the region of the eastern border of Arizona," etc., he fails to give credit where credit is due. What actually occurred was this:

About the eighth or ninth of October, late in the afternoon, my Mexican mule herder came to the hacienda in great excitement and reported that he had been fired at by Indians, who had then driven off our herd of team mules, fifty-three mules and a bell mare. With my American ranch foreman and seven Mexican ranch hands, armed, except the foreman and myself, with nondescript guns of ancient patterns, I followed the trail and ascertained that the Indians were headed north and would cross the American line near the New Mexico-Arizona border.

I sent one of my men to the railroad with a telegram to Miles stating what had happened, the direction the Indians were taking, and my opinion that they were heading for the Reservation. On this information Miles, as he says, ordered Captain Charles L. Cooper of the Tenth Cavalry with twenty enlisted men and two scouts from Fort Apache to proceed in search of them.

Encumbered with my old wagon mules the Indians made slow progress, were encountered in an open flat, made no resistance, and were readily captured,—thus to Captain Cooper goes the credit of the only actual *capture* of armed Indian *men* during the entire campaign. A month later fifty-one of the mules were returned to me under escort of Lieutenant Johnson, a courtesy on the part of General Miles that I sincerely appreciated.

The terms Miles authorized Gatewood to offer Geronimo's band, and under which Gatewood induced them to surrender, were that they "were to be sent *with their families* to Florida." The italics are mine to call attention to a clear breach of a treaty of peace on the part of our officials that, through his high sense of honor, embittered the rest of Gatewood's life. The principal reason that Nachite, in particular, decided to surrender, and that caused him to influence Geronimo, was the desire and belief that he was soon to see his family again. But instead of being sent to Florida *with their families,* as they were led to believe, the men of the hostile party were confined in the dungeons of Old Fort Pickens at Pensacola and their families at St. Augustine in Fort Marion, several hundred miles away.

Nor was this the only outrage perpetrated on these people. At Fort Apache were some seventy-five men and about 325 women and children who had resisted all efforts of the hostiles to induce them to leave the Reservation. Moreover, every adult male, almost without exception, had served at some time as a scout in pursuit of the hostiles, nearly all of them serving six months or more. With every inducement and influence to turn on their officers, they had remained faithful and had given of the best in them. Without them the subjugation of the hostiles would have taken years and countless lives.

Yet at Fort Apache, by order of Miles, under direction of the officials in Washington, Colonel Wade suddenly surrounded them with troops, Miles having sent there for this purpose four troops of cavalry to reinforce the three troops of cavalry and two companies of infantry stationed there. The men were disarmed and they with the women and children sent to Fort Marion; the same punishment that was meted out to the hostiles themselves.

It must be said in justice to General Miles that he

opposed the plan to send these people to Fort Marion and advocated their being located in Indian Territory, but was told that the law in reference to the establishment of Indian Territory prohibited it. Miles then suggested Fort Union, New Mexico, but was advised by the Washington authorities that no proposition looking to the location of the Chiricahua and Warm Spring Indians west of the Missouri River could be entertained.

Later the indignant protests of Mr. Herbert Welsh, Secretary of the Indian Rights' Association, and other prominent persons who investigated the condition of these people and the terms of Geronimo's surrender, forced the Washington authorities to unite the families and send them first to Alabama and later to Indian Territory, where the remnants of them are today.

My former comrade and friend, the late Captain John G. Bourke, Third U.S. Cavalry, in his *On the Border With Crook* closed his account of General Crook's Indian services with an expression of our feelings in this matter far better than I can express them myself.

Not a single Chiricahua had been killed, captured, or wounded throughout the entire campaign—with two exceptions—unless by Chiricahua-Apache scouts who, like Chato, had kept the pledges given to General Crook in the Sierra Madre in 1883. The exceptions were: one killed by the White Mountain Apache near Fort Apache, and one killed by a white man in northern Mexico. Yet every one of those faithful scouts—especially the two, Ki-e-ta and Martine, who had at imminent personal peril gone into the Sierra Madre to hunt up Geronimo and induce him to surrender—were transplanted to Florida and there subjected to the same punishment as had been meted out to Geronimo. And with them were sent men like Goth-kli and Toklanni, who were not Chiricahua at all, but had only lately married wives of that band, who had never been on the warpath in any capacity except as soldiers of the Government, and had devoted years to its service. There is no more disgraceful page in the history of our relations with the American Indians than that which conceals the treachery visited upon the Chiricahua who remained faithful in their allegiance to our people. An examination of the documents cited will show that I have used extremely mild language in alluding to this affair.

Following the surrender of the hostiles, General Miles made his headquarters in Los Angeles. Some months later the citizens of Tucson gave a banquet in his honor. At the banquet he was presented with a Tiffany sword and Lawton with a fine watch for "capturing Geronimo."

Gatewood had been invited to the dinner, but was detailed in command of the post while Miles and the other officers were away. His reward came later. Returned to his regiment, he was put on sick leave for a year in the hope of restoring his health, broken by eight years of service in the field with Indian scouts. Shortly after rejoining his regiment at Fort McKinney, Wyoming, a barracks in the post caught fire, threatening the destruction of the entire post. In an attempt to blow up one of the buildings to save the others, a premature explosion of dynamite shattered one of his arms and so thoroughly completed his disability that he was retired on the half pay of a first lieutenant, with a wife and two small children to provide for.

He died in May, 1895, and his widow, with her children still to rear, was granted the munificent pension of seventeen dollars a month.

THE Order of Indian Wars, with headquarters at

Washington, is a small association primarily of officers of the army who have taken part in Indian campaigns. They meet at least once a year for a dinner and reminiscences, publishing later in pamphlet form for distribution among the members an account of the meeting and such papers in relation to Indian affairs as have been read or submitted at the meeting.

In the published account of the dinner held January 26, 1929, there is included an account of the Geronimo Campaign by Brigadier General James Parker, U.S. Army, Retired. I could not close this account of the Capture (?) of Geronimo more fittingly than with these extracts from General Parker's article.

"Early in June, 1886, General Miles arrived at Fort Huachuca. To get an idea of the country he and I climbed to the summit of El Moro mountain near the post. I have never been slow at suggestions and I took this opportunity to ask General Miles if I could make one.

" 'I have recently come from Fort Apache where the Chiricahuas not with Geronimo are located,' I said. 'Whenever there is news of a raid, the Chiricahuas, in order not to become involved in the fighting, go into the post and are quartered in the quartermaster corral.

" 'I would suggest a false report of a raid be spread and when the Indians are in the corral, they be surrounded by the troops, disarmed, taken to the railroad and shipped east as prisoners of war. Geronimo's band in the field will then be isolated, will no longer receive aid and comfort, as heretofore, and will surrender.' 'Why that would be treachery,' said the General. 'I could never do that.' . . . But nevertheless it was only a few weeks later when the Chiricahuas at Fort Apache, being assembled to receive rations, were surrounded by troops, disarmed and sent by railroad to Florida. This was in August. In September, Miles, in his negotiations with Geronimo, used this fact to bring about the surrender."

IN HOC SIGNO VINCES: Which in this instance might be freely translated BY THESE MEANS WE CONQUERED THEM.

FINIS

Index